D0626045

GOA BEACHES

ENCOUNTER

AMELIA THOMAS

Goa Beaches Encounter

Published by Lonely Planet Publications Pty Ltd
ABN 36 005 607 983

Australia	Head Office, Locked Bag 1, Footscray, Vic 3011 ☎ 03 8379 8000 fax 03 8379 8111 talk2us@lonelyplanet.com.au
USA	150 Linden St, Oakland, CA 94607 ☎ 510 250 6400 toll free 800 275 8555 fax 510 893 8572 info@lonelyplanet.com
UK	2nd fl, 186 City Rd London EC1V 2NT ☎ 020 7106 2100 fax 020 7106 2101 go@lonelyplanet.co.uk

This book was written by Amelia Thomas. It was commissioned in Lonely Planet's Melbourne office and produced by: **Commissioning Editors** William Gourlay, Shawn Low, Suzannah Shwer **Coordinating Editor** Katie O'Connell **Coordinating Cartographer** Jacqueline Nguyen **Assisting Cartographers** Xavier Di Toro, Alex Leung, Marc Milinkovic **Layout Designer** Jacqui Saunders **Assisting Editor** Kate Evans **Managing Editors** Imogen Bannister, Katie Lynch **Managing Cartographers** David Connolly, Adrian Persoglia **Cover** Image research provided by lonelyplanetimages .com **Project Manager** Chris Girdler **Managing Layout Designer** Sally Darmody **Indexer** Saralinda Turner **Thanks to** Helen Christinis, Frank Deim, Joshua Geoghegan, Laura Jane, Chris Lee Ack

ISBN 978 1 74179 430 4

Printed through Colorcraft Ltd, Hong Kong.
Printed in China.

Mixed Sources
Product group from well-managed forests and other controlled sources
www.fsc.org Cert no. SGS-COC-005002
© 1996 Forest Stewardship Council

FSC

HOW TO USE THIS BOOK
Colour-Coding & Maps

Colour-coding is used for symbols on maps and in the text that they relate to (eg all eating venues on the maps and in the text are given a green knife and fork symbol). Each neighbourhood also gets its own colour, and this is used down the edge of the page and throughout that neighbourhood section.

Send us your feedback We love to hear from readers — your comments help make our books better. We read every word you send us, and we always guarantee that your feedback goes straight to the appropriate authors. The most useful submissions are rewarded with a free book. To send us your updates and find out about Lonely Planet events, newsletters and travel news visit our award-winning website: *lonelyplanet.com/contact*.

Note: We may edit, reproduce and incorporate your comments in Lonely Planet products such as guidebooks, websites and digital products, so let us know if you don't want your comments reproduced or your name acknowledged. For a copy of our privacy policy visit *lonelyplanet.com/privacy*.

AMELIA THOMAS

Amelia Thomas is a British writer and journalist who works throughout India and the Middle East, often with her highly understanding husband and excitable four under-fives in tow. She has worked on numerous Lonely Planet guides, and her research trip to Goa unintentionally became longer-term when her family decided they liked it so much, they'd stay for the season. Her book, *The Zoo on the Road to Nablus*, telling the true story of the last Palestinian zoo, was published in 2008, and she is currently working on *Hypnosis!* – a tale of the life of eccentric Goa native and hypnotist extraordinaire, Abbé Faria (see p78). Her ideal day involves a long walk along Agonda Beach (p108) and a dip in the sea at Palolem (p110); her toddlers, however, would argue that a close encounter with a troupe of monkeys, a long sandcastle session, and several 'Raspberry Dolly' ice creams make the perfect Goan combination.

AMELIA'S THANKS

Thanks, first, to Pinky and her wonderful family, and to Nich and Cheryl for sunset G&Ts and breakfast *bhaji-paus* (small, spicy curries with a fluffy bread roll for dunking). Many thanks to Will Gourlay, Shawn Low, Sam Trafford and the Lonely Planet team, and, as always, to Gal, Cassidy, Tyger, Cairo and Zeyah, without whom I'd be lost – even in Goa.

THE PHOTOGRAPHER

Greg Elms has been a contributor to Lonely Planet for over 15 years. Armed with a Bachelor of Arts in Photography, Greg was a photographer's assistant for two years before embarking on a travel odyssey. He eventually settled down to a freelance career in Melbourne, and now works regularly for magazines, graphic designers, advertising agencies and, of course, book publishers such as Lonely Planet.

Cover photograph Local women walking along Arambol Beach, Travel Ink/Getty Images. **Internal photographs** p47, p64, p73, p104, p117 by A Thomas. All other photographs by Lonely Planet Images, and by Greg Elms except p21 by Clint Lucas; p22 by Paul Harding; p24, p28 by Eddie Gerald.

All images are copyright of the photographers unless otherwise indicated. Many of the images in this guide are available for licensing from **Lonely Planet Images:** www.lonelyplanetimages.com

How now brown cow: a local resident works on its suntan on Palolem Beach (p110)

CONTENTS

Why is our travel information the best in the world? It's simple: our authors are passionate, dedicated travellers. They don't take freebies in exchange for positive coverage so you can be sure the advice you're given is impartial. They travel widely to all the popular spots, and off the beaten track. They don't research using just the internet or phone. They discover new places not included in any other guidebook. They personally visit thousands of hotels, restaurants, palaces, trails, galleries, temples and more. They speak with dozens of locals every day to make sure you get the kind of insider knowledge only a local could tell you. They take pride in getting all the details right, and in telling it how it is. Think you can do it? Find out how at **lonelyplanet.com**.

THIS IS GOA

Swaying palms, white sands and sparkling waters: the three essential elements that attract two million visitors to Goa's balmy shores every year are bountiful in this tiny, glorious slice of India that hugs the country's western coastline.

For almost 500 years Goa was a solitary Portuguese outpost in India, and the influence of colonial rule can still be seen almost everywhere: in the exquisite, crumbling architecture; in the East-meets-West cuisine, which combines coconut milk, palm vinegar and chillies with the refined flavours of Lisbon; in the melancholy strains of fado that still waft occasionally on the bougainvillea-scented breeze; and in the siesta-saturated *joie de vivre* that Goans call *susegad,* or *sosegado.*

Nowhere else in India will you find the laid-back languidness of a Goan lunchtime, the easy charms of its people, or the soothing serenity of a day on its beaches. In Goa, a herd of water buffalo will greet you at breakfast, a lily-covered lake might provide the scenery for a morning walk, a sea eagle will prove an afternoon companion along a deserted stretch of pristine beach, a gorgeously spice-laden *vindalho* can make your evening repast, and a fiery glass of cashew-palm feni liquor will be your bedtime tonic.

Whether you choose to ply the state squeezed sardinelike into its faithful chugging buses or opt, as most travellers do, to buzz its byways on a scooter or aboard a roaring Royal Enfield motorbike, the more you explore the more you'll love this little haven in the maelstrom that is India. Wander its riotous markets, experience a blazingly colourful Muslim, Hindu or Catholic festival, then lie back and relax with a sunset cocktail or an ayurvedic massage on its glorious beaches, where coconut palms murmur gently overhead and crabs scuttle silently in the shallows.

So come, shed your cares, and be intoxicated by the hospitality that's kept invaders of both the friendly and more forceful varieties returning time and again for centuries.

Top left Colonial architecture on show at Hospedaria Venite (p82), Panaji **Top right** Time out on Mandrem Beach (p40) **Bottom** Colourful culinary delights prepared street side

ARABIAN SEA
Colva
Madgaon
Madgaon
Curtorim
Chandorgoa
Sanvordem
Sanvordem
Sanguen River
Benaulim
Chandor
Sanguem
Varca Beach
Varca
Chinchinim
Quepem
Cuncolim
Assolna
Orlim
Cavelossim
Cavelossim Beach
Mobor
Mobor Beach
Betul
Bali
0
10 km
0
5 miles
ELEVATION
600m
300m
150m
50m
0
Cabo da
Rama Fort
Cola Beach
Barcem
Agonda Beach
Agonda
Butterfly Beach
Palolem
Palolem Beach
Chaudi
Patnem
Canacona
Rajbag Beach
Rajbag
Talpona
Galgibag Beach
Galgibag
Poinguinim
Cotigao
Wildlife
Sanctuary
Masher
To Polem
Beach (2km)

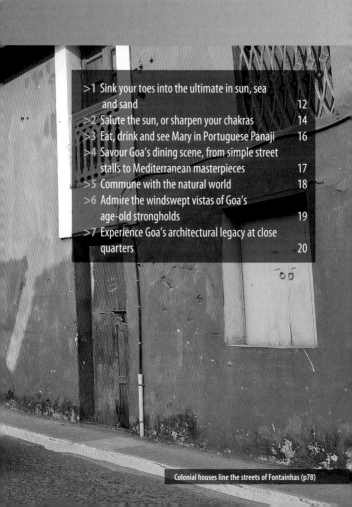

Colonial houses line the streets of Fontainhas (p78)

>1 SOUTHERN GOA'S SILKEN SHORES

SINK YOUR TOES INTO THE ULTIMATE IN SUN, SEA AND SAND

In a diminutive state seemingly so tightly packed with beachfront development, it's astoundingly easy to escape the tourist crowds and find your own patch of sand-based paradise. This is nowhere easier than in south Goa, by far the least developed of the state's seaside stretches and with miles of sand on offer to satisfy your every Robinson Crusoe fantasy.

Within minutes of even the most buzzing of south Goan resorts, you're sure to find beachside bliss if you know where to look. From busy Colva (p98), strike up north to the tiny villages of Majorda (p95) and Betelbatim (p96), where a scattering of five-star resorts has actually helped keep smaller-scale shoulder-to-shoulder development at bay. Here you'll find sea birds wheeling over empty stretches of sand; solitary swimmers striking out to sea; and the occasional palm-thatched beach shack to provide a seafood lunch, a cool lime-soda or a hot, sweet glass of chai.

Likewise, past busy Benaulim (p100) and Cavelossim (p101), you'll encounter undisturbed golden sand that stretches south to the

mouth of the River Sal at Mobor (p102), where itinerant fisherfolk haul in their wares and the Blue Whale beach shack (p103) graces one of the most picture-perfect spots in all of Goa.

Further south from Mobor, a trip across the languid Sal on a rust-bucket passenger ferry will take you to solace and solitude on magnificent Agonda Beach (p108; pictured above) with its wide swathe of sand, and to a quiet, laid-back scene at little Patnem (p116), at which point Goa's beach development largely ends. South from here is Galgibag (p121), the almost sole preserve of sea eagles, dolphins and endangered Olive Ridley turtles, and then Polem (p121), Goa's southernmost beach, which, though beautiful, sees few daytrippers hitting its sands – perhaps due to its reputation as a smugglers' stronghold for locally produced moonshine.

But even if you are looking for something with more of a pulse, you'll rarely be confronted down south with ranks of sun loungers. The star of the southern show remains Palolem (p110), without doubt one of the state's most beautiful bays, which retains its charms despite the unbroken ranks of beach shacks and coco-huts. A safe swim, a hearty lunch and a sunset that lights up the heavens – how much closer to perfection could it get?

>2 EXPLORING ANCIENT HEALTH REGIMES

SALUTE THE SUN, OR SHARPEN YOUR CHAKRAS

This small, sunny state has become, in recent years, one of the country's most bountiful destinations for yoga and meditation, along with almost any other form of spiritual health regime or therapy you could toss a yoga mat at. From an hour's active ashtanga (a fluid and challenging form of yoga; the basis for 'power yoga') to 10 silent days of vipassana (an intensive, silent, inward-looking form of meditation), you'll find activities in abundance, with practitioners an ever-changing parade of foreigners who set up shop as soon as the monsoon subsides, and offer their services to the scores who come seeking enlightenment, illumination or any spark of spiritual something.

By far the most popular of the myriad regimes on offer in Goa is ayurveda, the ancient science of plant-based medicine, whose Sanskrit name comes from a combination of *ayu* (life) and *veda* (knowledge). Illness, in the doctrine of ayurveda, comes from a loss of internal balance, which can be restored through a combination of massage and *panchakarama* (internal purification).

The first part of the regime comprises an hour-long rub-down with warm medicated oils, followed by a cleansing steam bath. This

sort of massage is available almost anywhere in Goa, though it's best to go by local recommendation to seek out the very best ayurvedic hands on offer.

The second, internal purification part takes rather more than an hour, and most people opt for a fortnight's course of treatment in order to feel its advantages. In this case, your cure will comprise of a carefully tailored diet, exercise regime and a series of treatments to supplement your massages. For most of us, intent on finding our balance aboard a sunbed, the hour-long treatment inevitably wins out as most appealing.

Second only to ayurveda in Goa is yoga, in all its various guises. Try your hand at ashtanga or hatha (gentler and slower paced), Iyengar (slow and steady, often using blocks and straps) or vinyasa (built around a sun salutations sequence), to find the pose and poise that suits you best.

And Goa's commitment to the well-being of its visitors doesn't stop there. Take a vipassana retreat (p40), lay your hands on a spot of reiki (healing through the laying-on of hands), or seek out t'ai chi, Zen Buddhism, belly dancing, sacred drumming circles, tarot, palmistry or healing colour therapies. It's all here in balmy – and sometimes barmy – Goa.

>3 PICTURESQUE PANAJI

EAT, DRINK AND SEE MARY IN PORTUGUESE PANAJI

As India's state capitals go, Goa's towers above the rest, as calm and composed as its others are seething and stressful. Bearing the distinct imprint of Portuguese rule, it's the perfect place for a day away from the beach. Wander along meandering streets still lined with gorgeous colonial relics (pictured above), complete with bright pots of geraniums, peeling paint, and cages of songbirds gracing shady balconies.

Stretching out lazily along the banks of the broad Mandovi River, Panaji (p78) first rose to prominence in 1843, when it replaced disease-plagued Old Goa (p88), just a quick paddle upstream along the river, as regional capital. Nowadays it's the destination of choice for a spot of shopping in one of its chic 'lifestyle' stores; for dipping into a fine selection of atmospheric restaurants; and for catching a flick or two at the annual November International Film Festival of India (p24).

But a visit to Panaji isn't complete without a visit to either the city's dazzlingly frothy 16th-century centrepiece, the Church of Our Lady of the Immaculate Conception (p78), or a tipple at one of its countless cubby-hole bars: the pinnacles of saintly, or sinful, sightseeing.

>4 FINE ECLECTIC DINING

SAVOUR GOA'S DINING SCENE, FROM SIMPLE STREET STALLS TO MEDITERRANEAN MASTERPIECES

From the moment you wake until the hour you drop off to sleep, the scents and flavours of Goa's cuisine will rarely, if ever, elude you. Start the day the Goan way with a simple *bhaji-pau* (a small, spicy curry with a fluffy bread roll for dunking; pictured above) and a sweet cup of chai tea, then move on to lunch at a chic Mediterranean bistro, and top it off beneath the stars with a freshly grilled seafood extravaganza.

Goa's beaches, meanwhile, teem with every cuisine under the sun, and whether you're craving a good goulash or a perfect pizza you'll likely find it somewhere here, while a bevy of top-end choices whip up some incredible upscale culinary experiences.

At the other end of the spectrum, simple South India treats abound, and a hearty lunch can easily be had for less than a dozen rupees. Dosas (rice-flour pancakes), *idlis* (steamed rice cakes) and *vadas* (deep-fried lentil-flour doughnuts), along with lassis (thick yoghurt-based shakes) are just a few midmorning treats, while the traditional local dish of fish-curry-rice (fried mackerel in spicy, soupy sauce) fires up Goans for the afternoon's work – or siesta – ahead. Arrive willing to explore and experiment, and prepare to be thrilled by the adventurous palette on offer to the adventurous palate.

See also p126.

>5 GLIMPSING GOA'S FASCINATING FAUNA

COMMUNE WITH THE NATURAL WORLD

Even if you're not one to jump at the sight of a pangolin or puff-throated babbler, the chances remain high that you'll soon be charmed by Goa's charismatic collection of indigenous species, both of the wild and domestic inclinations.

Ply any of the shady lanes that snake alongside Goa's beaches and you'll encounter noble herds of oxen and water buffalo, plodding home in long, faithful family herds. Villages, too, are teeming with animal life, from darting black piglets to obstinate silver langur monkeys, from glancing geckos to cavorting kittens. At night, flocks of bats emerge flapping from Goa's manifold church eaves; during the day, you'll catch the ultramarine flash of a kingfisher in a lush paddy field, watch snow-white egrets hopping a ride on board their bovine buses, and see hawks, vultures and eagles hovering high overhead.

Goa's seas are ripe for spotting pods of dolphins – which frequently swim up so close to shore that you need nothing more than a sharp pair of eyes to sight them – while its underwater world appeals to divers, who might be rewarded with sightings of parrotfish, stingrays and sea turtles. The Mandovi's famous crocodiles, also known as 'muggers', meanwhile, can be viewed at a safe distance on 'croc-watching' trips, as can its more peaceable birdlife, with avian-rich trips available from many beaches for the truly tenacious twitcher. See also p131.

>6 INVADING CRUMBLING CLIFFTOP FORTS

ADMIRE THE WINDSWEPT VISTAS OF GOA'S AGE-OLD STRONGHOLDS

Strategically dotted along Goa's coastline stand the overgrown, crumbling forts that once defended an empire as it clung tightly to its lucrative piece of the spice trade on the Arabian Sea. Taking a trip along narrow rural seaside lanes in search of these relics is one of the most memorable ways of exploring Goa's coastline and, on a clear day, usually affords unbeatable views.

Built of long-lasting laterite stone and strengthened to perfection to prevent enemies from breaching their defences, Portugal's far flung bastions for centuries bore down on would-be trade rivals, their thick walls built to deflect even the most determined cannon shot. But as the threat of sea attacks diminished during the 18th and 19th centuries – with savvy invaders choosing a terrestrial rather than a waterborne route – Goa's forts fell into a long, slow decline. Most today are evocative shadows of their former selves, their once invincible walls now breached by encroaching creepers.

Seek out decrepit Cabo da Rama (p108) in south Goa, tucked away behind miles of lush coconut groves, or Fort Aguada (p70; pictured above) further north, to peruse the best-preserved example of Portugal's power and Asia's oldest lighthouse. Admire the views from bleak Chapora Fort (p51), or stay a night in Terekhol Fort (p40) at the very top of the state, for your very own taste of Portugal's once unbeatable maritime might.

HIGHLIGHTS

>7 CHECKING IN TO A HISTORIC HERITAGE HOTEL

EXPERIENCE GOA'S ARCHITECTURAL LEGACY AT CLOSE QUARTERS

Goa's wealth of colonial architecture has, in recent years, prompted the creation of numerous 'heritage' hotels (such as Siolim House, pictured above), heavy on a winning combination of atmosphere and luxury. Dotted throughout both tourist centres and traditional local villages, set back from the sea and shaded by lush gardens, these small, select sanctuaries make the perfect place to hide out in style for a night or two, dipping in and out of shimmering courtyard pools, dining at high table, revelling in the individual attention that only a small hotel can afford, and perhaps indulging in a spa treatment or two.

But even for those not intent on checking in, there are plenty of places to check out the state's architectural highlights. In Candolim (p68), for example, a meander along shady back lanes will throw up a host of hidden, still-inhabited 18th-century *palaços* (palaces). But to get a true insight into the history lurking behind the ornamental pilasters, carved pediments and oyster-shell windows, step back in time with a trip through Candolim's Calizz (p70). Here, Goa's homes are brought to life by historian-guided tours, who point out the function behind the frills and folderols. That way, when you lie back and admire your heritage hotel's architecture from your perfect poolside perch, you'll know exactly what you're looking at.

See also p124.

>GOA BEACHES DIARY

When it comes to festivals, Goans enjoy any excuse to party and barely a week goes by without a *festa* illuminating the calendar. These range from dignified deific celebrations to huge and raucous street parades, especially exuberant and feni-fuelled during the Carnival that hits Panaji annually on the run-up to Lent. Goa's religious diversity means that Christian, Hindu and Muslim events are observed with equal aplomb, and that some religious festivals, such as Christmas and Shigmotsav, are celebrated by everyone, regardless of their creed. For updates on festivals with movable dates, check the Goa Tourism Development Company's online resource, www.goa-tourism.com.

Golden times at Goa Carnival (p22)

GOA BEACHES DIARY

JANUARY

Reis Magos Festival

Held on 6 January, most notably at Reis Magos Church (p84), this festival sees a re-enactment of the Three Wise Men's journey to Bethlehem, with young boys playing the Magi and white horses providing their transport.

FEBRUARY

Shigmotsav (Shigmo)

Goa's take on the Hindu festival of Holi takes place over the full-moon period to mark the onset of spring, and sees state-wide parades, processions and revellers flinging huge quantities of water and coloured tikka powder with wild abandon.

Carnival

Mirth and mayhem characterise Goa's annual Carnival, held on the three days prior to the onset of the Catholic calendar's Lent. Festivities come to a head in Panaji on Sabado Gordo (Fat Saturday), with a procession of floats through the city's packed streets. See also p136.

MARCH & APRIL

Easter

Churches fill up state-wide over the Christian festival of Easter, with plenty of

Procession for the Feast of the Three Kings held during the Reis Magos Festival

High Masses and family feasting thrown in for good measure.

JUNE

Feast of St Anthony

This feast in honour of Portugal's patron saint, held on 13 June, takes on particular significance if the monsoon is late in appearing, in which case each Goan family must lower a statue of the saint into its family well to hasten the monsoon's onset.

Sanjuan

The Feast of St John (or *Sanjuan*, in the local Konkani dialect) on 24 June sees young men diving dangerously into wells to celebrate the monsoon's arrival. The torching of straw dummies of the saint represents John's baptism and, in consequence, the death of sin.

Sangodd

The Feast of St Peter on 29 June marks another monsoonal celebration, particularly ebullient in Candolim, when boats are tied together to form floating stages and costumed actors play out *tiatrs* (Konkani dramas) to vast crowds.

SEPTEMBER

Ganesh Chaturthi

This Hindu festival in September celebrates the birth of elephant-god Ganesh. Effigies of the deity of peace and prosperity are displayed in elaborate shrines, then paraded through the streets to be immersed in the sea.

OCTOBER & NOVEMBER

Feast of the Menino Jesus

On the second Sunday in October, coastal Colva's village church sees its small and allegedly miracle-working statue of the infant Jesus paraded before scores of devoted pilgrims.

Diwali

The five-day Hindu 'festival of lights' celebrates the victory of good over evil with the lighting of oil and butter lamps about the home, lots of gentle familial celebration and plenty of less peaceful firecrackers.

GOA BEACHES DIARY

Christmas decorations adorn Panaji's Church of Our Lady of the Immaculate Conception (p78)

International Film Festival of India

www.iffi.gov.in

This film festival – the country's largest – graces Panaji's big screens each November, with a gaggle of Bollywood's finest glitterati jetting in for premieres, parties, ceremonies and screenings.

DECEMBER

Feast of Our Lady of the Immaculate Conception

On 8 December, Panaji's wedding-cake Church of Our Lady of the Immaculate Conception (p78) plays host to a feast and a large, joyful fair.

Christmas

Midnight masses abound in Goa on 24 December – traditionally known as *Misa de Galo*, or 'Cock's Crow', since they often stretch on far into the wee hours. Christmas Day itself is celebrated with feasting, fireworks and festivities by locals and tourists alike.

Sunburn Festival

www.sunburn-festival.com

For the last couple of years, 'Asia's biggest music festival' has set up camp in Candolim over Christmas and New Year. Check the website for details, and if it continues to run to form, you'll find a four-day dance-music extravaganza filled with international DJs and all-day partying.

Shower time: visitors get a trunk full at a Ponda spice farm (p119)

ITINERARIES

Plans in Goa are footloose and fancy-free, and each new, sun-drenched morning invites you to decide, on a whim, how you'll spend it. The pleasure lies in taking time to discover your own hidden haunts, so here are some suggestions, without a tight schedule or carefully timed itinerary in sight.

ONE DAY

If you're only in Goa for a day, make like a local with a breakfast *bhaji-pau* (a small, spicy curry with a fluffy bread roll for dunking) in a tiny local roadside cafe, then hit the beach all day to revel in the sand and surf you've been longing for. Linger over a leisurely beach-shack lunch, retire for a lazy Goan siesta, then sip cocktail concoctions whilst watching the sun sink slowly into the sea. Dine in seafood splendour on the sands, and look out for shooting stars whilst heading to bed amid the croaks and creaks of a million tree frogs and cicadas.

TWO DAYS

Start your second day stretching, with a yoga session (p14) beneath swaying coconut palms, then head out for a water-borne daytrip in search of a pod of dolphins, teeming birdlife, or a languid family of river crocodiles (p131). After dinner, don your best bargaining head to score a bargain amid the stretch of street stalls extending down to your nearest beach, and shop for hand-embroidered bed sheets, hammocks, silver jewellery or vintage trinkets (p134).

THREE DAYS

On day three, hop on your scooter to explore the coast's enchanting country lanes, dodging off wherever takes your fancy to find that deserted strip of beach for a quick, refreshing dip. Let your nose be your guide to a fish-curry-rice (fried mackeral in a spicy, soupy sauce) lunch (p126), then head up to a historic fort (p19) for stunning coastal views, poking your nose into a few village churches as you wind your way homeward for a colourful take on Christianity (p130). Ease away the pains of the road with

---

Top left Indulge in Café Chocolatti's (p74) tranquil garden setting **Top right** Parasailers over Sinquerim Beach (p72)
Bottom Satisfy your inner shopaholic at Goa's plethora of roadside market stalls

an ayurvedic massage and steam bath (p14), then trawl the beach bars in search of live music, or the promise of a party (p136).

A FAMILY DAY

Fill up on finger-licking dosas and sweet banana lassis for breakfast, then take a morning trip by taxi out to a spice farm (p119), to ride on an elephant, eat from banana-leaf plates and sniff the sweet scent of vanilla straight from the pod. Hit gently shelving Palolem Beach (p110) with

An intricate carving of the Virgin Mary stands inside Old Goa's Sé Cathedral (p88)

FORWARD PLANNING

Three weeks before you go Check for forthcoming festivals or plan a couple of whirlwind daytrips with the Goa Tourism Development Corporation (p151). Reserve an ultimate dose of romance by organising an outing with Faraway Cruises (p118). Book tickets for a swish Christmas or New Year gala celebration at the Intercontinental Goa Lalit or Leela Kempinski (p125) if you're Christmassing in the sun.

One week before you go Reserve a table for dinner at Baga's Le Poisson Rouge (p66) or J&A's (p66). Brush up on a few phrases of the local Konkani dialect to elicit a smile during those hard-bargaining shopping encounters. Listen online to a spot of Luis de Miranda (p141) to get yourself into the fado-infused mood.

The day before you go Telephone or email your hotel to double-check they're expecting you; fill your spare luggage space with useful items to aid Goa's orphan children or stray animals (p128). Check out what's going on in Goa, online, with a peek at the local newspaper (www .oheraldo.in).

bucket and spade in the afternoon, then wander up to its northernmost point to wade out across the river and watch crabs scuttling in the rock pools at sunset. After dark, head to Patnem's Magic Cinema (p118) for an outdoor movie and a simple supper.

A DECADENT DAY

Indulge in breakfast at Candolim's Café Chocolatti (p74), then laze the morning away stretched out on Sinquerim's sands. Wander back down the beach for an exquisite lunch at Republic of Noodles (p75) and spend the afternoon shopping in the boutiques and international-name chains of Calangute and Baga, before dining at Calangute's A Reverie (p61). Work off the calories at Baga's legendary Tito's (p67), where you can get your groove on, Ibiza-style, until the early hours.

A BUSY DAY

Drag yourself from the beach for a wander through the picturesque Portuguese-style streets of Panaji (p78), to soak up the old-world atmosphere and trawl its stores. Hop over to Old Goa (p88) for a glimpse of what was once the 'Rome of the East', then pass by Colva Beach (p98) for an adrenalin-boosting jet-ski or parasailing ride. Head home via Majorda for a sunset horse ride along the sands (p96), and top it off by indulging in some old-fashioned cooking (and a bit of energetic karaoke) at Betelbatim's Martin's Corner (p97).

>BEACHES & TOWNS

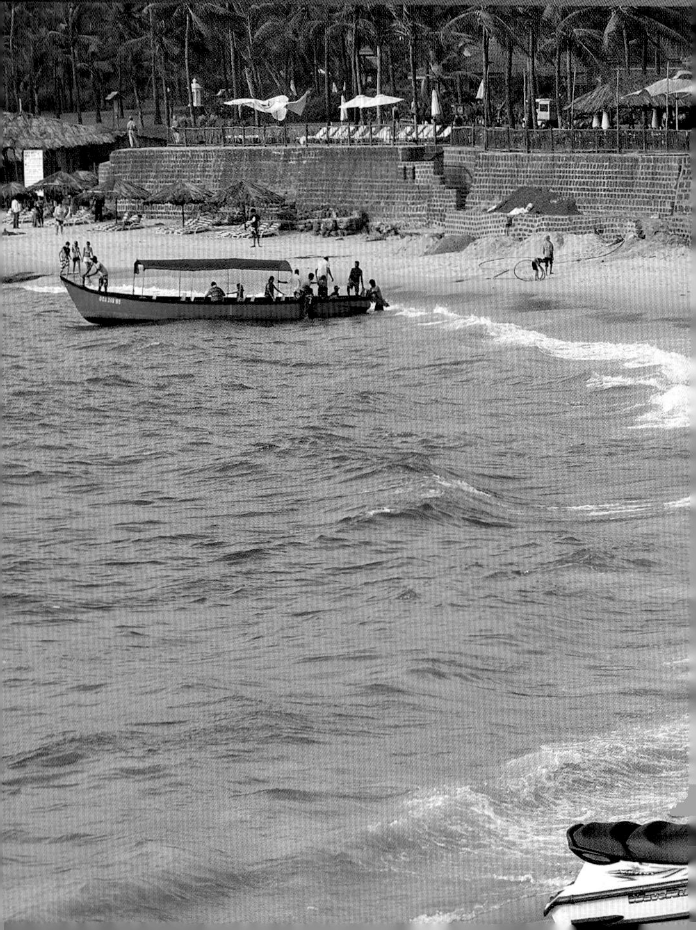

Water sports aplenty on Sinquerim Beach (p72)

BEACHES & TOWNS

Where you decide to position your beach blanket, book and bikini during your stay in this little sandy paradise depends very much on precisely how much, or how little, you intend to do when you get here.

Very generally, Goa can be divided into three distinct regions: north, central and south. The north, above the Mandovi River, is the place for those seeking action, shopping and activities in equal supply, and for folks looking for the remnants of Goa's fabled trance-party scene. The north also boasts some big beaches, a string of highly developed resorts, and lots of choice in restaurants, hotels, nightlife, shopping and water sports.

In central Goa, between the Mandovi and Zuari Rivers, things get decidedly more cultural. Here sits Panaji (also known as Panjim), Goa's small state capital, which offers yet more great shopping and dining amid beautiful Portuguese colonial architecture. Inland lie the glorious remnants of Goa's grand but fatally flawed ecclesiastic past at Old Goa, along with some quiet backwater islands, which offer a taste of Goa's pastoral yesteryear.

Things slow down even more in the south, where the beaches are quieter and the sun loungers are spaced further apart. Not generally the place for partying the night away, the south caters to a quieter, calmer crowd, with lots of homespun charm and pristine countryside. This is the place to sit back, unwind, and spot a hatching turtle or two, before saddling up your moped and heading back up the twisting seaside lanes to the bright lights and big beaches of the north.

It's important to note that outside cities such as Panaji and Mapusa, many destinations shut up shop for the monsoon season, roughly between mid-May and late October. If you visit during this time, you'll find resorts deserted, boat trips on hold, and restaurants running on restricted opening hours – but this is not necessarily a bad thing. During the monsoon rains, Goa's countryside becomes even more emerald than usual, and the lack of visitors sees rare wildlife creeping out of the woodwork. Beaches are yours to explore, hotel prices are halved, and the local welcome is perhaps even warmer than usual; just remember to pack your umbrella.

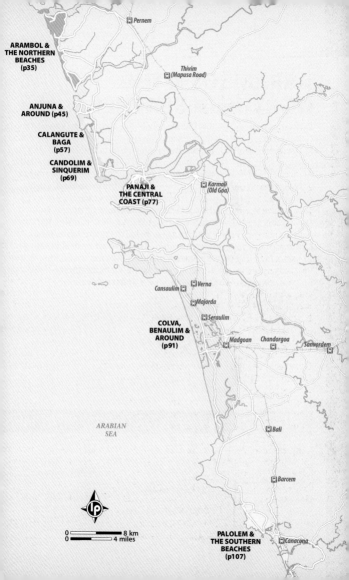

Pernem

Thivim (Mapusa Road)

Karmali (Old Goa)

Cansaulim

Verna

Majorda

Seraulim

Madgoan

Chandorgoa

Sanvordem

Bali

Barcem

Canacona

ARABIAN SEA

0   8 km
0   4 miles

>ARAMBOL & THE NORTHERN BEACHES

Goa's rocky, cove-filled northernmost stretch, wedged in between the broad Terekhol and Chapora Rivers, is largely the preserve of independent travellers, who flock to the budget beach huts that line the Arambol cliffside, and to the ever-increasing slew of barefoot luxury operations ranged along the wide, largely empty sands of Aswem and Mandrem.

Mandrem, in particular, has of late become the preserve of yoga enthusiasts, with classes and retreats appearing in their dozens every year, whilst Morjim, to the south, is home to two distinct breeds: long-staying Russian tourists, and endangered Olive Ridley turtles, the latter coming in to land several times a year to lay their eggs on its sands. At Goa's northernmost tip perches little Querim, a laid-back alternative to Arambol for a day or two of beach lounging. Beyond it is historic Terekhol Fort, accessible by rusting ferry and offering the opportunity, these days, for a luxurious stay entirely free from the threat of invasion.

ARAMBOL & THE NORTHERN BEACHES

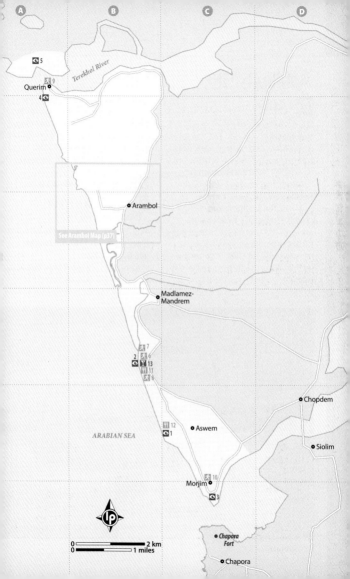

V

BEACHES & TOWNS

ARAMBOL & THE NORTHERN BEACHES

ARAMBOL

👁 SEE

⬡ ARAMBOL BEACH

Map opposite

Also known as 'Harmal', Arambol has been backpacker-central since the heady '60s, and remains a low-key, low-budget destination, teeming with cheap beach-hut accommodation and basic beach-shack cafe-restaurants. Though its 'alternative' scene has turned a touch too mainstream for hardcore hippies, it nevertheless remains the largest and most popular of Goa's far-northern resorts. Its main covelike beach is gently curved and safe for swimming, perhaps the reason why, in recent years, Arambol has become popular among families with young children, who hang out happily among the uniformly dreadlocked, tattooed and creatively pierced individualists.

🏃 DO

🏃 HIMALAYAN IYENGAR YOGA CENTRE *Yoga*

Map opposite; www.hiyogacentre.com; 5-day courses Rs 2500; ⏲ courses mid-Oct–mid-Mar

This place – the seasonal headquarters of a centre based in the North Indian Himalayan foothills –

Blissed out: Arambol Beach is the centre of Goa's backpacker scene

ARAMBOL

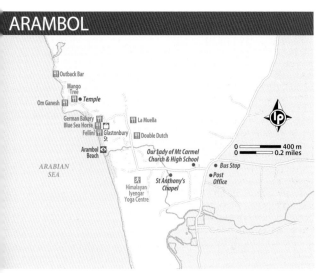

...s a popular place for a spot of yoga, with five-day courses for all levels of practitioners, intensive workshops, Sunday afternoon children's classes, and teacher training all available. The centre is situated south of Arambol's main beach strip, about 500m from St Anthony's Chapel.

TAKE A WALK Walk

At low tide, it's a leisurely and picturesque 3km walk north along the beach, past a freshwater lagoon and on to the quiet sands of Querim (p39), where you can cool off with a dip in the sea and a cold beach-shack beer before heading back again. Alternatively, a 4km stroll south down the beach will bring you to marvellously mellow Mandrem (p40).

SHOP

GLASTONBURY STREET
Market Stalls

Map above; 9am-11pm

Everything beaded, mirrored, embroidered and embellished is to be found on the stretch of sandy lane winding down to the beach that British festival-going visitors refer to as 'Glastonbury Street'. Here, stalls jostle shoulder-to-shoulder to sell you everything Indian, so haggle hard to fill your bag with bright and beautiful bed spreads, bindis, *bidis* (local, hand-rolled cigarettes) or bongos to take back home.

EAT

▯ BLUE SEA HORSE
International $$
Map p37
Situated just where beach meets street, Blue Sea Horse serves a solid all-day menu with extensive seafood options when the catch comes in, but its popularity soars come sunset, with mean cocktails and a nightly movie (usually screened around 7pm) on offer.

▯ DOUBLE DUTCH
International $$
Map p37
An ever-popular option for its steaks, salads and backpacker-famous apple pies, this is a great place to peruse the noticeboard for current Arambolic affairs, whilst munching on a plateful of cookies or a huge, tasty sandwich.

▯ FELLINI *Italian* $$
Map p37
A long-running Italian joint, perfect for when you're craving a carbonara or calzone, Fellini delivers all your wood-fired pizza and

fresh pasta requirements in the thick of the Arambol action.

▯ GERMAN BAKERY
Breakfast, Bakery $
Map p37; ⏱ **7am-late**
This rather dim and dingy corner cafe beneath the Welcome Inn hotel is particularly popular with Israeli travellers, and is worth a pit stop for its lemon-cheese pie and scrummy chocolate-biscuit cake, as well as its big, big breakfasts.

▯ LA MUELLA
International, Vegetarian $$
Map p37
A woodsy ambience and great vegetarian food are the flavours of the day at this nice little place, with especially good hummus courtesy of the Israeli owner-cook.

▯ MANGO TREE *Beach Shack* $$
Map p37
A calm, colourful set-up with an extensive menu, cushions for those lazy moments, and a pool table for more active ones; Mango Tree's a great place to cool down, chow down or, as it proclaims itself, chill out.

▯ OM GANESH *Beach Shack* $
Map p37
Rush here just before sunset to garner one of a few tiny tables within splashing distance of the

waves, or sit back and enjoy the view from a drier aspect. This place sports a pages-long menu offering almost every cuisine under the sun: try a tasty Tibetan *thukpa* (noodle soup), or while away the hours decoding more cryptic entries, such as the Mexican '*Gokomadi*'.

OUTBACK BAR *Seafood* $$
Map p37
Seafood is a speciality at this nice place tucked safely back from the Arambol action; it also makes a fantastic spot for a sundown cocktail or two.

QUERIM

◉ SEE

◉ QUERIM BEACH
Map p35
Quiet Querim is the place to come to while away the hours in peace and tranquillity, with only the occasional beach shack for company. Backed by a shady cover of fir and casuarina trees – though sadly this hinterland is becoming a little litter-blown – there's not much to do here but have a leisurely swim, settle back with a book and revel in the tranquillity that descends so

Enjoy a view of the Terekhol River and Fort Terekhol (p40) from these sun lounges

VIPASSANA – THE ART OF SILENCE

Chances are that during your Goan sojourn you'll see vipassana courses on offer, and wonder what exactly they involve. Vipassana, roughly meaning 'to see things for what they really are', is a meditation technique most often taught in Goa as a 10-day residential retreat, concentrating on 'self-transformation through self-observation'. In practice, this translates as 10 days of meditation, clear thought and near silence, abstaining from killing, stealing, lying, sexual activity and intoxicants, and concentrating at length on one's own breathing. Sounds like your cup of decaffeinated tea? Consult www.dhamma.org for more detailed information.

close, yet so far, from the Arambol action.

◉ TEREKHOL FORT
Map p35; ◷ 11am-5pm

As north as north Goa goes, this historic bastion just across the river from Querim was built by the ruling Maratha dynasty in the early 18th century. It was soon taken by the Portuguese, against whom a failed mutiny was attempted here by a plucky Goan governor-general in 1825. Nowadays, part of the fort has been transformed into the small, luxurious and far more peaceable Fort Tiracol Hotel (p125), while the rest is opened up daily for the public to poke about in, including the opportunity to peek into its glum little Chapel of St Anthony.

🏃 DO
🏃 QUERIM FERRY *Ferry*
Map p35; pedestrian/motorbike/car free/Rs 4/10; ◷ 7am-10pm

If you're planning on a trip up to Terekhol Fort (left), it's fun to hop on board the Querim ferry that chugs passengers and vehicles across the Terekhol River from the end of the village every 30 minutes. If you find yourself stranded at low tide on the opposite side – when services are suspended for several hours – head downstream several kilometres to a second ferry point, and wind your way through a surreal amber landscape of iron-ore mines.

MANDREM

◉ SEE
◉ MANDREM BEACH
Map p35

Mandrem is, for many, the best-kept secret on the north Goan coast, as laid back and languid a destination as you could possibly hope for. Yoga, meditation and ayurveda are the orders of the day, and you'll find ever-changing options for spiritually slanted exercise and enlightenment along its sands. Head here for a day or two of beach-bound bliss, and you might find it hard to tear yourself away. Most accommodation, dining and alternative therapy options are ranged along the narrow beach-access road, or on the sparkling sands themselves.

 # DO

🏃 AMALIA CAMP
Alternative Therapies
Map p35; www.neeru.org
Its slogan – 'Meeting Yourself' – might give you a clue as to what's going on at Amalia Camp, situated just north off the beach access road, where local guru Neeru hosts *satsangs* (devotional speech and chanting sessions) to help ease you toward that ever-elusive Enlightenment. Her own personal three-point plan invites you to join her in 'Step One: Realisation of Truth; Step Two: Liberation of the Mind; Step Three: Integration into Life'. Check her website for forthcoming opportunities to do so.

🏃 ASHIYANA RETREAT CENTRE
Alternative Therapies, Yoga
Map p35; ☎ 9850401714; www .ashiyana-yoga-goa.com; ☾ Nov-Apr
This 'tropical retreat centre', situated right on Mandrem's beach, has a long list of classes and courses available, from retreats and yoga holidays to daily drop-in workshops, meditation and yoga sessions, along with a spa, massage, and 'massage camp' for those wanting to learn the tricks of the tickly trade. Its largely organic vegetarian restaurant dishes up tasty buffet brunches and dinners daily to guests and droppers-in alike.

🏃 FABULOUS BODY CARE
Alternative Therapies
Map p35; ☎ 9420896843; Oasis Restaurant; massage from Rs 800; ☾ 9am-8pm
Ayurvedic massage is to be had here, just behind Oasis Restaurant at the southern end of the beach, from the delightful Shanti, whose claim to fame is having massaged Dawn French. Try the rejuvenating 75-minute massage and facial package, or go for an unusual 'Poutli' massage, using a poultice-like cloth bundle containing 12 herbal powders, which is dipped in warm oil and comes especially recommended for back pain.

🍴 EAT

🍴 CUBA RETREAT
International $$
Map p35
Operating a chain of popular, laid-back beach bars, huts and restaurants all along the Goan coast, the Cuba folks claim to serve up

Extend yourself with a yoga class at Ashiyana Retreat Centre (p41), Mandrem

'exorbitant seafood delicacies' here in their relaxed courtyard bar-restaurant – though the prices seem more than reasonable to us. You'll find Cuba on the south side of Mandrem's beach-access road.

DRINK
SHREE GOPAL SUPREME PURE JUICE CENTRE & CAFE
Drinks, Snacks
Map p35; ⏱ **7am-10pm**
On the northern side of the road down to the beach, thirst-quenching juicy combinations are squeezed and served up in a cute little chill-out area. Lots of notices

are posted on trees, lamp posts and boards in the vicinity, offering information on the latest retreats and yoga-class locations.

ASWEM
SEE
ASWEM BEACH
Map p35
A wide stretch of quiet beach backed by a rather lacklustre village strip, the quiet Aswem sands are popular with long-staying foreigners and play host to an annually changing parade of beach-hut

THE TURTLE WIND

Each November, a strong breeze known as the 'turtle wind', heralds the arrival of Olive Ridley marine turtles to lay eggs on a clutch of Goan beaches including Morjim. It's believed that these females – who live more than a century – return to the beach of their birth to lay eggs, often travelling thousands of kilometres to do so.

Recently, Olive Ridley numbers have plummeted due a host of human-created hazards, and they're now protected by Goa's Forestry Department, which operates information and protection huts on Morjim, Agonda and Galgibag Beaches. Drop into these, or go to www .goaforest.com to learn more.

accommodation and beach-shack restaurants. Though some stretches of the beach are becoming distressingly grubby, development here is generally low-key, swimming is usually safe, the sands are quiet, and the vibe, very mellow.

EAT

LA PLAGE *Mediterranean* $$

Map p35; ☽ lunch & dinner

Renowned among Aswem's many beach-shack offerings is La Plage, which for the last six seasons has been dishing up sumptuous gourmet Mediterranean food in simple surroundings, concocted by a genuine French chef.

MORJIM

SEE

MORJIM BEACH

Map p35

A tiny, bleak beachfront village at the mouth of the Chapora River, Morjim is the destination of choice for long-staying Russians, many of whom rent whole houses and settle in for the season. It's worth a visit to brush up on your Cyrillic, paddle á la Black Sea, wander the riverbanks and admire the views of Chapora Fort (p51) on the opposite side, and perhaps glimpse endangered Olive Ridley turtle hatchlings, who emerge from their eggs here (in sadly ever-decreasing numbers; see left) between October and March.

DO

YOGA VILLAGE

Alternative Therapies, Yoga

Map p35; ☎ 2244546; www.yoga village.org; 2-week retreat €800

If you're in need of a serious spiritual fine-tuning, a two-week retreat at Yoga Village might be just what the doctor ordered. Prices include ayurvedic meals, cottage accommodation, yoga and daily metaphysical discussion. The village is situated in a jungly clearing, and is a little difficult to find; call for detailed directions.

>ANJUNA & AROUND

Almost everyone in Goa has heard stories of Anjuna, that bastion of all things hippy and home to one of India's most famous weekly markets. Until recently, nearby Vagator, too, had quite a reputation, as Goa's centre for the fabled, drug-fuelled Goa trance parties which attracted thousands of revellers to all-night jungle raves.

Things, however, have quietened down considerably of late. Anjuna's hippies have largely upped sticks and left for South Asian pastures new, whilst Vagator's trance scene, much to locals' relief, has been virtually halted by 'noise pollution' laws, demanding that all parties be shut down by 10pm.

Nowadays, though the odd party persists and drugs are still there for the taking, Anjuna and Vagator are slowly moving upmarket, with boutique hotels creeping in to replace former hippy hovels. Meanwhile, tiny northerly Chapora remains a centre for dedicated smokers, where the heady scent of charas (cannabis or hashish) hangs thick in the air, whilst lovely Siolim, a short hop inland, makes for an interesting foray into local village life.

ANJUNA & AROUND

🔵 SEE
Anjuna Beach 1 B5
Chapora Fort 2 B1
Chapora Harbour 3 B1
Chapora Village
  Centre 4 B1
Little Vagator Beach 5 A2
Ozran Beach 6 B4
Vagator Beach 7 A2

🏠 SHOP
Andy's Tattoo Studio 8 B5
Anjuna Flea Market 9 B6
Oxford Arcade 10 B4
Orchard Stores 11 D4
Rainbow Bookshop 12 B2

🍴 EAT
Avalon Sunset 13 B5
Bean Me Up Soya
  Station 14 C3
Café Diogo 15 C5
Café Orange Boom 16 C5
China Town 17 B2
German Bakery 18 C6
Mamma Mia 19 C2
Mango Tree Bar and
  Cafe 20 B2
Maria's Tea Stall 21 C6
Marrakesh 22 B3
Martha's Breakfast
  Home 23 C5
Munches 24 B4
Om Made Cafe 25 B5
Whole Bean 26 C5

🍸 DRINK
Alcove Resort 27 B3
Beach Bars 28 B6
Casa Anjuna 29 B4
Casa Vagator 30 B2
Laguna Anjuna 31 C4
Sai Ganesh Fruit Juice
  Centre 32 C5
Scarlet Cold Drinks 33 B3

⭐ PLAY
Hilltop 34 B3
Nine Bar 35 A2

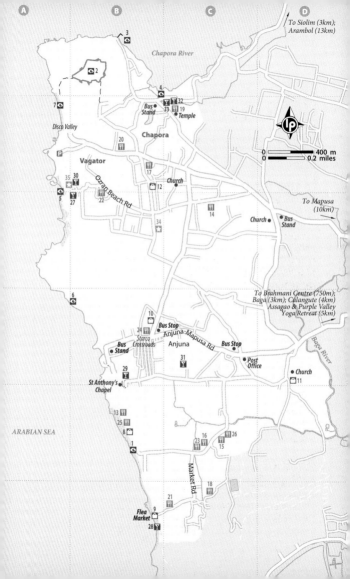

ANJUNA

SEE

ANJUNA BEACH

Anjuna Beach, extending south from the village centre to the flea market site and beyond, makes a pretty and surprisingly quiet place for a stroll or a game of frisbee, though swimmers should be aware of a powerful undertow. At low tide, the northern portion of the beach gets submerged by the waves, and fills up with domestic tourist ladies hoisting up their saris and hopping precariously from rock to rock, in search of a scenic photo opportunity. Following the clifftop path south from the village will take you past lines of cafes, cell block–style guest-house rooms and market stalls, before depositing you gently down onto the sands just beside San Francisco Restaurant. South from the flea-market site, however, the sands become mournfully blighted with rubbish and engine oil: avoid this patch for both sea- and sun-bathing purposes.

DO

BRAHMANI CENTRE *Yoga*

www.brahmaniyoga.com; classes Rs 500, 10-class pass Rs 3500; ☼ **Nov–Apr**
This friendly drop-in centre, in the grounds of Anjuna's Hotel Bougainvillea (also known as Granpa's Inn; see p125), offers daily classes in ashtanga, vinyasa, hatha, dynamic, kundalini, restorative and, intriguingly, 'Superhero Acro-Flow' yoga, as well as pranayama meditation. There's no need to book: just turn up 15 minutes before the beginning of class to secure space enough to spread your yoga mat.

PURPLE VALLEY YOGA RETREAT

Alternative Therapies, Yoga

☎ **2268364; www.yogagoa.com; 142 Bairo Alto, Assagao; 1-week courses from £390**
Based in Assagao village, this popular retreat, set amid frangipani-scented tropical gardens, offers one- and two-week residential courses in ashtanga yoga; rates include accommodation and delicious all-vegetarian meals. A range of beauty therapies and ayurvedic treatments are also available on-site for course participants.

YOGA, REIKI & AYURVEDA

Alternative Therapies, Yoga

Anjuna teems with drop-in yoga classes, reiki circles and sessions, and ayurvedic treatments. Ask around locally for the season's best bets, or consult notice boards at Café Diogo (p49), Café Orange Boom (p49) or the German Bakery (p49).

Anita Edgar
Co-founder/Director of El Shaddai child-rescue charity (p129)

How did your charity begin? I came here in 1996 to recharge my batteries after driving aid trucks for 15 years. Three days into my holiday, I saw some little homeless children, fending for themselves, near my hotel. That day, God gave me a vision to open homes to help these children. **What's the most rewarding thing about your work?** To rescue a child from a tragic situation, and when they come to you with their exam results or admission to university, to know that without our help, they would be dead. **And the hardest?** Endless bureaucracy, and the fact that most holidaymakers just aren't aware of the terrible lives these children lead. **How can foreigners best help?** Sponsor a child with one of Goa's children's charities (see p128). It costs about £25 per month to give them everything, and offer a desperate child the chance of life.

🛍 SHOP

🛍 ANDY'S TATTOO STUDIO
Tattooing

**www.andys-tattoo-studio-anjuna-goa
.com;** 🕐 **11am-7pm Sep-Apr**

Shop for a more permanent sort of souvenir next door to the San Francisco Restaurant, just where the Anjuna cliffside slides down to meet the beach. Andy embellishes shoulders, ankles and everything in between – drop in to make an appointment.

🛍 ANJUNA FLEA MARKET
Market Stalls

🕐 **8am-late Wed**

Without doubt the most important date in the Anjuna diary, market day sees scores of local and expat vendors descending on the market site at the far south of the beach, to haggle the day away over clothing, jewellery, souvenirs and a good deal, these days, of usual tourist tat. Pick through the rubbish (underfoot, quite literally) to seek out treasure, including sparkling ceiling hangings, dancing dolls, and posh frocks made from dazzling saris. Even if you don't come home loaded with shopping, it's an unmissable event, where you'll find Goa's old faithful hippies mingling with I Heart Goa–clad Indian tourists, package-holiday Brits and Russians, and young backpackers in search of bargain.

🛍 ORCHARD STORES
Groceries

Stocking all the comforts of home, this small and jam-packed (in both senses of the phrase) village shop dispenses familiar grocerial all-and-sundry to those in need of Heinz baked beans, Marmite or proper pesto, washed down with a nice glass of Ribena.

🛍 OXFORD ARCADE *Groceries*

Just next to the Starco Crossroads, the Oxford Arcade is a fully fledged supermarket, complete with shopping trolleys, ice-cold air conditioning, and check-out scanners. Hallowed ground for self-caterers who pay dearly for lit-

Haggle hard at Anjuna Flea Market

le luxuries, it also sports a bakery, toiletries department, pet food, wine department and children's toys. Come Christmas, this is the place to buy your tinsel and baubles, fake tree, and kids' gifts to stack beneath it.

EAT

🍴 AVALON SUNSET
International $

www.avalonsunset.net
Good food, a pool table, a chill-out area and free wifi make this a great representative of Anjuna's clifftop restaurant parade. There's daily yoga on the roof, too; call in for class times.

🍴 CAFÉ DIOGO *International* $

🕑 **breakfast & lunch**
Probably the best fruit salads in the world are sliced, diced and served with honey and fresh curd at Café Diogo, a small locally run place on the way down to the market. Also worth a munch are the mean fry-ups; the generous toasted avocado, cheese and mushroom sandwiches; and an unusual gooseberry lassi (yoghurt shake).

🍴 CAFÉ ORANGE BOOM
International $

🕑 **breakfast & lunch**
Just past Café Diogo, on the opposite side of the road, this nice

little place has the same good food and friendly service at similar prices, with a useful notice board for catching up on Anjunan goings-on.

🍴 GERMAN BAKERY
International $$
Lovely, leafy and filled with prayer flags and jolly lights, this is a perfect place for a huge lunch, selected from a huge menu, while lounging back on huge floor cushions. Tofu balls in mustard sauce with parsley potatoes and salad is a piled-platter pleaser; wifi is available for Rs 100 per hour.

🍴 MARIA'S TEA STALL
Snacks, Drinks $

🕑 **Wednesday**
Colourful elderly local Maria doles out piping-hot chai, tasty samosas, and a decent rendition of a falafel salad sandwich each Wednesday, from dawn to dusk, from her tiny stall in the thick of the flea market (opposite). Speak up, though: she's often engrossed in exchanging village gossip with her friends.

🍴 MARTHA'S BREAKFAST
HOME *International* $$
As the name suggests, Martha's speciality are her breakfasts, served up in a quiet garden on the way down to the flea-market site.

The porridges and juices might be mighty tasty, but the star of the breakfast parade is undoubtedly the piping-hot plates of waffles, just crying out to be smothered in real maple syrup.

🍴 MUNCHES *International* $$

🕐 **24hr**

Near the Starco Crossroads, this ever-popular place, serving up the full list of travellers' favourites, is a good choice for whenever any attack of the munchies demands you munch.

🍴 OM MADE CAFÉ *International* $$

🕐 **8.30am-sunset**

The highlight of Anjuna's entire clifftop strip, this chic and cheery little place offers striped deckchairs from which to enjoy the views and the simple, sophisticated breakfasts, sandwiches and salads. Go for a raw papaya salad with ginger and lemongrass, accompanied by a chickoo and coconut smoothie or a glass of 'perfumed water'.

🍴 WHOLE BEAN *Vegetarian* $$

🕐 **breakfast & lunch**

The Bean, the Whole Bean and Nothing but the Bean is served in myriad combinations at this simple, tasty health-food cafe – which proudly announces itself as 'Anjuna's premier soy destination'. It focuses on all things sweet and savoury, solid and liquid, and tempeh and tofu, created from that most versatile of legumes.

🍸 DRINK

🍸 BEACH BARS *Beach Bars*

South along the seafront from Anjuna's flea-market site, you'll find a cluster of beach bars hugging their sadly pollution-blighted sands. Shiva Valley and Curlies are two of the current favourites which really rev up for watering-hole action on market day, especially towards sunset; both occasionally see the action heading on into the wee hours and beyond.

🍸 CASA ANJUNA *Hotel Bar*

www.casaboutiquehotels.com

Part of the Casa chain, which operates some half-dozen boutique abodes state-wide, Casa Anjuna's beautifully restored colonial mansion makes for a lush and restful place to escape the market frenzy, and sip from a chilled glass of chardonnay whilst examining your purchases.

🍸 LAGUNA ANJUNA *Hotel Bar*

www.lagunaanjuna.com

Even if the food's not up to much at languid Laguna Anjuna, its shaded terrace makes a great place for a cold drink – though spray yourself liberally with repellent to avoid becoming food for mosquitoes the

ize of mice. There's a pool table
inside the mansion-turned-bar
for shooting a frame or two, and a
sophisticated, old-world feel that
makes it a joy to imbibe here.

SIOLIM

SEE

VILLAGE CENTRE
Pretty Siolim makes an interesting
stop-off, whether to gaze at its
numerous colonial-mansion mas-
terpieces or simply to experience
its slice of small-town life. Peep
into its 16th-century St Anthony
Church, one of the oldest Christian
shrines in Goa, and jostle with
locals amid its two small bazaars;
one, fishy flavoured, congregates
daily on the banks of the Chapora
River, while the second is held
early on Wednesday mornings
around central St Anthony's.

CHAPORA

SEE

CHAPORA FORT
Perched high on a hill above the
headland, Chapora's red-laterite
fort has surveyed the surrounding
scene for the last four centuries, having been built by the
Portuguese in 1617 on the site
of an older Muslim construction.

According to local legend, it fell to
the Hindu Marathas in 1739 with
the help of some rather tenacious
monitor lizards, who clambered
the steep fortress walls like living
crampons, while supporting the
invading warriors' weights.

CHAPORA HARBOUR
The narrow road northwest of the
village leads past lots of village
homes with rooms for rent, up to
a small harbour where the day's
catch is hauled in from colourful,
bobbing fishing boats. Self-
caterers with the desire for fresh
fish can haggle for their supper
direct with fisherfolk, while for
most others, it's a scenic photo
opportunity and an interesting
window into traditional village life.

VILLAGE CENTRE
Though the wild trance parties of
yesteryear may be as much a thing
of the past as day-glo, Chapora's
heady, hippy scene soldiers on,
its little village centre filled with
assorted misfits and miscreants,
making it strangely reminiscent of
Star Wars' Mos Eisley Cantina. It's
a favourite with charas smokers,
who appear to be little disturbed
by the powers-that-be: simply
stand around at the ancient central banyan tree for a few minutes,
amid the bongs and chillums, to
catch a whiff of what's floating
along on the sea breeze.

BEACHES & TOWNS

ANJUNA & AROUND

 # EAT

MAMMA MIA *Italian* $$

8am-9pm Tue-Sun

Though plenty of poky places pepper the main village strip, the best Chapora choice by far is Mamma Mia, run by an Italian, Marco, who makes his own focaccia fresh every night in preparation for the next day. The cappuccinos are perfectly frothy, the pizza is simple and filling, and the smoke, as almost everywhere in Chapora, is heady.

 # DRINK

SAI GANESH FRUIT JUICE CENTRE *Drinks, Snacks* $

Offering similar stuff to Scarlet (below), in equally close proximity to the thickest gusts of smoke, this diminutive juice centre is a great place for a vitamin fix and a fascinating spot for people-watching.

SCARLET COLD DRINKS
Drinks, Snacks $

Vending juice, lassis and snacks to munchies-driven travellers, a rickety table at Scarlet offers a perfect vantage point from which to observe Chapora's comings and goings; there's also an extremely useful noticeboard, pinned to bursting with news of the latest local yoga classes, reiki courses and the like.

WHERE'S THE PARTY?

Though Goa was long legendary among Western visitors for its all-night, open-air Goan trance parties, a central government 'noise pollution' ban on loud music in open spaces between 10pm and 6am has largely curbed its often notorious party scene. With a tourist industry to nurture, however, authorities tend to turn a blind eye to parties during the peak Christmas–New Year period, and seem to allow the monster mainstream clubs of Baga (p67) to carry on regardless. If you're looking for the remainder of the trance-party scene, however, you'll need to ask around; leap on anyone handing out flyers in Anjuna, Chapora and Vagator, and keep your fingers crossed for a musical miracle.

VAGATOR

 # SEE

LITTLE VAGATOR & OZRAN BEACHES

Vagator's sands are spread over three separate coves, of which the two southernmost are accessible by steep footpaths running down from nearby Nine Bar (p55). Both make upbeat, and sometimes cramped, places for a beach-shack lunch, a snooze on a sun lounger or a dip in the sea. With shacks dominating the sands, Goa Trance heavy on the sound systems, and cows thronging among the people, there's a distinctly laid-back and backpackerish vibe, all overseen by the huge, happy, carved Shiva face that gazes out from the Ozran rocks.

 VAGATOR BEACH
This beautiful stretch of sand, which has the benefit of good swimming, is the northernmost and largest of the Vagator beaches and only fills up for a few hours

each afternoon when domestic coach tours unload their swift-clicking tourist hoards. Avoid this time of day, and you'll have plenty of room for lounging on its pretty, boulder-studded sands.

 SHOP
RAINBOW BOOKSHOP
Books
☎ 2273613; ⏱ 9.30am-10pm
This lovely little backstreet place, run by a charming elderly gentleman, stocks a good range of second-hand and new books, including Lonely Planet's own.

🍴 EAT
🍴 **BEAN ME UP SOYA STATION**
Vegetarian $$
A delicious, all-vegetarian, court-yard restaurant graces this popu-lar guest house on the road from Vagator towards Mapusa, with lots of carefully washed salads and a wealth of tasty tofu and tempeh. Paid wifi is available (purchase vouchers at the guest-house reception), to surf whilst you sup.

🍴 **CHINA TOWN** *International* $$
Brightly painted and dispensing traveller favourites from its long menu, this simple place offers good chow meins and sweet-and-sours, as well as some decent seafood catches.

Best face forward: Vagator Beach

WORTH THE TRIP

The bustling, workaday town of Mapusa, situated around 7km from both Anjuna and Ca-langute, is northern Goa's largest town, and makes a great place to get a quick glimpse of urban Goa's goings-on. It's home to the state's liveliest local market, **Mapusa Market** (☼ 8am-sunset), which is most worthwhile visiting on Friday, when throngs of locals arrive to vend fresh produce, clothing, textiles, bangles and footwear, along with more tourist-oriented jewellery, mirrored bed spreads and the like. Inside the market area, small cafes churn out chai and snacks at break-neck speed, and everyone haggles hard to score their bargain. If you're looking to buy – or are simply in the mood for a taste of local life – it makes a great place to meander.

When the market heat gets too much for you, **The Pub** (☼ 9am-10.30pm) is a great bet for watching the milling market crowds over a cold beer, or lunching on eclectic daily specials including roast beef and goulash with noodles. Don't be fooled by the dingy entrance or stairwell.

Meanwhile, for a windowless remnant of a more mahogany-clad era, the dingy **Casa Bela** (☼ 9.30am-3pm & 6-10.30pm), is a good place to escape the Mapusa blather and sip silently on a cold Kingfisher. The service is surly, but this only enhances the slightly bizarre charm of this little scrap of days gone by.

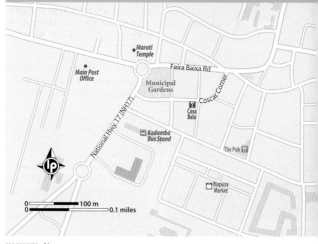

MANGO TREE BAR & CAFE
International $$

A perennially popular backpacker place, known for its generous breakfasts and far-ranging menu. Films are screened here most nights of the week, from 7.30pm or thereabouts.

MARRAKESH
Moroccan $$

Ozran Beach Rd; 11am-11pm
Billing itself as the 'Heart of Moroccan cuisine', this is the place to pick up a tasty tagine or a delectable vegetarian couscous, in what seems to be Goa's only Moroccan restaurant.

DRINK

ALCOVE RESORT *Hotel Bar*
www.alcovegoa.com
Situated a stone's throw from Nine Bar (right) atop the Little Vagator Beach headland, the Alcove's upbeat bar, complete with pool table, makes a great place for a sunset cocktail or a late-night drink, with picture-perfect views out over the charismatic Vagator coves.

CASA VAGATOR *Hotel Bar*
www.casaboutiquehotels.com
Within earshot of the noisy Nine Bar (right), the Casa Vagator boutique hotel might not be the most serene destination for an evening aperitif (unless, of course, you've an equal thirst for second-hand techno) but the decor makes up for the dance music. If you arrive for a nightcap after 10pm, you'll have the sound of cicadas, rather than clubbers, to keep you company.

PLAY

HILLTOP *Club*
sunset-late
Deserted by day, this place comes alive after nightfall, its out-of-town location allowing it on occasion (and for now, at least) to gleefully flout 10pm noise regulations to host concerts, parties and the occasional international DJ. Venture up to the site by day, and wander about until you find someone who'll tell you what's on, when.

NINE BAR *Club*
Sunset Point, Little Vagator Beach; till 10pm
Once the epicentre of Goa's trance scene, custom has cooled at the open-air Nine Bar, though the trance still thumps away each evening until it's turned off promptly at 10pm. On good nights, a trace of parties past can still be encountered; on bad, its atmosphere is akin to a wedding reception, long after the bride and groom have gone home.

>CALANGUTE & BAGA

Depending on your definition of fun in the sun, the twin resorts of Calangute and Baga – once the habitat of naked, revelling hippies and nowadays package-holiday central – can prove holiday heaven or the Bosch-like depths of Hell.

Calangute was once, long ago, the place to which well-heeled Goan townsfolk would retreat for a change of air, while Baga, to the north, remained a sleepy fishing village until well into the 1980s. These days, though, Calangute's and Baga's wide, continuous strip of sand sees relentless action, crowded with beach shacks, bars, water sports operators, hawkers, sun bathers and revellers of both the domestic and foreign varieties.

If you're coming to Goa seeking spiritual solitude, you'll find quite the reverse here, with Calangute's main beach drag being closer to Blackpool than Blissed-Out. But if you're looking for action, dance-around-your-handbag clubbing, exquisite cuisine and nonstop shops, with the occasional holy cow or temple elephant thrown in to remind you where you are, you couldn't hope for better.

CALANGUTE & BAGA

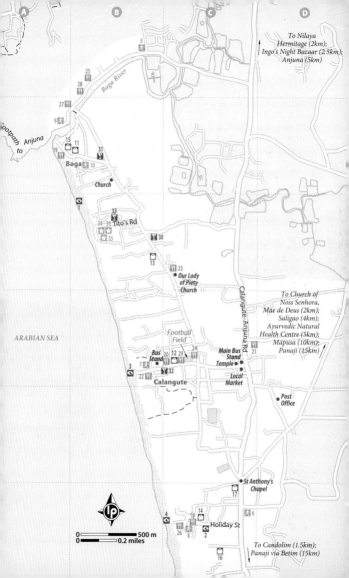

To Nilaya
Hermitage (2km);
Ingo's Night Bazaar (2.5km);
Anjuna (5km)

Baga River

25
28
27
9
15 11
19   31
Baga 10
     Church

33
34 36   Tito's Rd
35
         30
13

         23
      Our Lady
      of Piety
      Church

Footpath to Anjuna

ARABIAN SEA

Calangute-Anjuna Rd

To Church of
Noss Senhora,
Mae de Deus (2km);
Saligao (4km);
Ayurvedic Natural
Health Centre (5km);
Mapusa (10km);
Panaji (15km)

Football
Field

Bus
Stand
20 29
7 12 24
       32   21
22
Calangute

Main Bus
Stand
Temple

Local
Market

Post
Office

St Anthony's
Chapel
17

4
      18 14
26   3   8   2   Holiday St
                 6

16

To Candolim (1.5km);
Panaji via Betim (15km)

0   500 m
0   0.2 miles

CALANGUTE

◉ SEE

◉ CHURCH OF NOSSA SENHORA, MAE DE DEUS

Situated 2km from Calangute towards the village of Saligao, you can't miss this church as you explore the countryside, with its unusual neo-Gothic Christmas-cake style, topped with fanciful turrets. Built in 1873, it houses an allegedly miraculous statue of the Mother of God herself, and is illuminated brightly – making it a useful landmark for navigating the surrounding country lanes – each night.

◉ KERKAR ART COMPLEX

☎ 2276017; www.subodhkerkar.com; Holiday St; ⏱ 10am-11pm

Showcasing the colourful paintings, photographs and sculptures of local artist Dr Subodh Kerkar, this mellow little place makes a welcome break from the Calangute chaos.

◉ MAIN CALANGUTE BEACH

Calangute's main beach, along with the road leading to it, is India's 'Kiss Me Quick' capital, a kitsch delight of tacky souvenirs, cheap eats, dingy local bars, soft-serve ice creams, and milling, bewildered coach-tour visitors. Here you'll find touts vying for water-sports custom, buckets and spades being wielded with enthusiasm,

and plenty of wholesome seaside fun. Don't expect any kind of R&R but it's undeniably fun, if only for a Mister Softee–sized dose.

◉ SOUTH CALANGUTE BEACH

Far more sophisticated than its Main Beach counterpart (left), Calangute's south beach is the preserve of classier joints. Its sands are quieter (though by no means deserted), its restaurants are more upscale, and its pace altogether more relaxed. The south is the place for sundowners, shopping and sumptuous dining, away from the tourist tat a tad further north.

Kerkar Art Complex

Catch some rays on South Calangute Beach – just don't forget the sunscreen!

🏃 DO

🏃 AYURVEDIC NATURAL HEALTH CENTRE
Alternative Therapies, Yoga
☎ 2409275; www.healthandayurveda .com; Chogm Rd, Saligao
This highly respected centre, in the village of Saligao 4km inland from Calangute, offers a vast range of courses in reflexology, aromatherapy, acupressure, yoga and various other regimes. There's also a range of herbal medicines on offer and treatments available by an ayurvedic doctor.

🏃 DAY TRIPPER TOURS *Daytrips*
☎ 2276726; www.daytrippergoa.com;
🕐 9am-6pm Oct-Apr
With its head office based in south Calangute, this is one of Goa's best tour agencies, running a wide variety of day excursions out and about in Goa, along with multiday trips to locations further afield.

🏃 GOA TOURISM DEVELOPMENT COMPANY
Tours, Daytrips
GTDC; www.goa-tourism.com
GTDC daytrips (see p151), which depart regularly from Calangute

THE FUTURE OF GOA'S NIGHT MARKETS

Until recently, the highlight of any Calangute or Baga Saturday night came in the form of a trip to one of two local lively night markets: Mackie's Saturday Nite Bazaar and Ingo's Saturday Nite Bazaar, held each Saturday from 6pm to midnight and filled with vendors, street food, live music and garlands of fairy lights. During the 2008 to 2009 season, however, both were cancelled, though their grounds remained vacant, and opinion was divided on whether they might be reinstated. Ask around to find out, since they're well worth a shopping spree if they're up and running once more.

and offer tours of the Goan sights at a break-neck pace, can be booked at the front desk of the rather miserable Calangute Residency Hotel, just beside the Main Calangute Beach.

GURU BABA
Alternative Therapies, Yoga
Holiday St

Offering everything from an hour's massage to multiweek courses in yoga and meditation, this venerable old guru is to be found in a small shack on the western side of Holiday St. Ring the bell to call him; he's equipped neither with telephone nor email ('I heal the people who

use them,' he says sagely). Simply tell him your age and profession, and he'll instantly offer advice on which treatment regime is best for you.

SHOP

BOOK PALACE *Books*
☎ 2281129; 9am-7pm

Next to the football ground on the road to the beach, dusty old Book Palace has a good selection of reading material in many languages, including many titles on India and Goa.

CASA GOA *Lifestyle Store*
☎ 2281048

Casa Goa is a treasure trove of furniture, jewellery, textiles and home accessories housed in an old Portuguese mansion. Browse here for a pair of vintage-styled candlesticks, a cute picture frame or clothes by renowned Goan designer, Wendell Rodricks.

ETERNAL CREATION
Clothes, Accessories
www.eternalcreation.com; Holiday St

Stop in at Eternal Creation to pick up beautiful Australian-designed, fair-trade clothes, jewellery and children's wear, ethically produced in the northern Indian mountains by a multifaith workforce and sold here at this cheerful, colourful little store.

LITERATI BOOKSHOP & CAFE *Books*

☎ 2277740; www.literati-goa.com;
🕑 10am-6.30pm Mon-Sat

Tucked away down a dusty lane at the far southern end of Calangute is one of Goa's best beachside bookshops. Piles of good reads are stacked onto shelves throughout the owners' home, and there's a good line in strong Karnatakan coffee to keep you focused.

OXFORD BOOKSTORE *Books*

☎ 9326060647; www.oxfordbookstore
.com; 🕑 10am-7pm

Just opposite St Anthony's Chapel, this is a well-stocked and well-run branch of the countrywide bookshop chain, offering fiction and nonfiction alike at decent prices.

🍴 EAT

🍴 A REVERIE *Mediterranean $$$*

Holiday St; 🕑 **7pm-late**

A gorgeous lounge bar, all armchairs, cool jazz and sparkling crystals, this is the place to spoil yourself, with the likes of Serrano ham, grilled asparagus, French wines and Italian cheeses. Try the delectable forest-mushroom soup with truffle oil or go for a bowl of wasabi-flavoured guacamole, with home-made chips.

The inviting courtyard of A Reverie

VEGETARIAN DELIGHTS

Tens of millions of Indian vegetarians can't be wrong — and India offers the world's best breadth of choice for those who abstain from fish, flesh and fowl. Here are a few staples you'll see gracing most menus, perfect for tucking into a conscience-free lunch.

> *Aloo gobi* – potatoes and cauliflower in a thick masala sauce
> *Dhal makhani* – black lentils and red kidney beans cooked up in a rich creamy stew
> *Malai kofta* – vegetable dumplings steeped in a rich, sweet sauce
> *Tandoori paneer tikka* – Indian cheese coated in hot-and-sour paste, and oven-baked
> *Channa masala* – chickpeas simmered in a spicy curry sauce

CASANDRE

International, Goan $$

🕑 **9am-midnight**

Housed in an old Portuguese bungalow, this dim and tranquil retreat seems mightily out of place amid the tourist tat of Calangute's main-beach drag. With a long and old-fashioned menu encompassing everything from 'sizzlers' to Goan specialities, and a cocktail list featuring the good old gimlet, this is a loveable time-warp, with a pool table to boot.

COPPER BOWL *Goan* $$$

Pousada Tauma Hotel; 🕑 **lunch & dinner**
Cute boutique hotel Pousada Tauma is the venue for this intimate little open-air restaurant, which serves up delicious, coconut and spice-infused Goan cuisine in the copper bowls that have given the place its name. Try out a spicy *balchao* or coconutty *xacuti*, and revel in the romance of the candle- and fairy light–lit location.

DELHI CHAAT *Snacks, Drinks* $

🕑 **8am-late**

In the thick of the seaside action, this highly popular takeaway joint dispenses all manner of spicy, savoury snacks to the milling masses, as well as delicious hot, sweet chai.

INDIAN KITCHEN *Indian* $

🕑 **dinner**

Down-to-earth local cooking greets you at the colourful courtyard restaurant of this funky little guest house, which serves good, largely vegetarian grub each evening.

INFANTERIA PASTRY SHOP

Breakfast, Bakery $

🕑 **7.30am-midnight**

Next to the Sao João Batista church you'll find this scrummy bakery, loaded with home-made cakes, croissants and little flaky pastries. The noticeboard here is a hotbed for all things current and counter-current.

LE JARDIN
Mediterranean $$$
**www.le-jardin-goa.com; Holiday St,
South Calangute;** 🕑 **7pm-late**
Inhabiting a pretty garden a-
twinkle with candles, here you'll
find upscale international options
such as Norwegian smoked
salmon, grilled lamb chops, but-
terscotch crème brûlée, and an
extensive international wine list.

STREET FOOD STALLS
Snacks, Drinks $
🕑 **evenings**
Set up just past the Main Calan-
gute Beach car park, a bustling
collection of street carts serves
up fresh, filling and fast *bhel puri*
(a fried savoury snack with toma-
toes, onions and chillies), grilled
sweetcorn, masala omelettes
and other tasty snacks. Congre-
gate with locals to watch street
vendors rustle up a street-food
masterpiece.

🍸 DRINK
BARISTA *Coffee*
🕑 **10am-4am**
If you find yourself in need of
a cuppa, rest weary feet on the
pleasant terrace of this country-
wide coffee chain, which is open
till late, and kick back with a cap-
puccino or a frothier, fancier iced
coffee–based creation.

🍸 JERRY JOHN JONESIUS
Local Bar
JJJ; 🕑 **7am-10.30pm**
Largely the preserve of locals, JJJ is
a suitably dingy and atmospheric
bar, in a strip loaded with plenty
more of the same. Snacks and basic
Indian meals (from Rs 50) are also
available, if you need to line your
stomach with something more
substantial than feni (liquor distilled
from coconut milk or cashews).

⭐ PLAY

INDIAN MUSIC & DANCE
RECITALS *Music, Dance*
admission per person Rs 300;
🕑 **6.45-8pm Tue**
Held in the outdoor courtyard
of the Kerkar Art Complex (p58),
these soothing recitals seem a
world away from the brasher,
bolder side of Calangute, and offer
a little glimpse into local tradi-
tional music and dance forms.

BAGA

🔎 SEE
BAGA BEACH
Like Calangute's beaches further
south, Baga's not the place to
come for tropical tranquillity.
Though wide and roomy, Baga's
beach consists of jostling shacks,
peppered with water sports and

Shamim Khan
Professional magician and proprietor of Star Magic Shop, Baga (oppos

What do you do for a living? I'm a magician with a passion. **How long hav you been practising magic?** For 20 years, or maybe more – since I was a sm child back in Delhi. **And 20 years on, how many tricks do you know?** I'd s 1000, perhaps more. **What's your favourite?** A snooker cue ball, which be- comes five balls, then three, then four, then appears from my mouth, then n ear, then vanishes. But then, of course, there's the Magic Key, and the Indian Rope Trick…it's hard to choose just one. **What's the best thing about bein a professional magician?** My hobby is also my job – not many people can that. And magic makes people happy: I love making people happy. I've got my shops, as well as this stall every Wednesday at Anjuna Market (p48), and everyone always leaves smiling. What better job can you get?

boat-trip touts, and row upon row of sunbeds. The crowd here is young and excitable, the music's loud, and the atmosphere runs from cheerful to chaotic.

DO

BARRACUDA DIVING *Diving*
☎ 2182402; www.barracudadiving.com; Sun Village Resort, Baga

This longstanding diving school offers a vast range of classes, dives and courses, including a free 'Try Scuba' family session every Monday. It also runs 'Project AWARE' which undertakes marine conservation initiatives and annual underwater and beach clean-ups.

JUNGLE GUITARS *Courses*
☎ 9823565117; www.jungleguitars.com; courses Rs 55,000

If you've always been one to strum to your own tune, Jungle Guitars might just be the place for you. Fifteen- to 20-day courses will allow you to build your own very steel string or classical guitar from scratch, overseen by master guitar-builder, Chris. Courses include all materials and a case for the finished product.

WATER SPORTS *Water Sports*
You'll find numerous jet-ski and parasailing operators on Baga Beach, and it pays to compare

a few to find the most competitive rate. Parasailing usually costs around Rs 1500 per ride; jet skis cost Rs 900 per 15 minutes, and waterskiing can be had for about Rs 800 per 10 minutes.

SHOP

ALL ABOUT EVE *Clothing*
☎ 2275687

Just next door to Karma Collection (below), and owned and operated by the same proprietors, All About Eve stocks unusual clothes, bags and accessories, unlike any of the usual array you'll find on a beach-road stall.

KARMA COLLECTION
Lifestyle Store, Antiques
☎ 2275687

Beautiful home furnishings, textiles, ornaments, bags and sundry other enticing stuff – some of it antique – has been sourced from across India, Pakistan and Afghanistan and gathered at Karma Collection, which makes for a mouth-watering browse. Fixed prices mean there's no need to bargain, a welcome relief after a stint amid the hard-haggling stalls.

STAR MAGIC SHOP
Magic Shop
Whilst strolling both Calangute and Baga, you might spot a shop or booth promising to teach you

magic tricks in a startlingly brief two minutes. Stop off here to purchase tricks and illusions to thrill your great aunties and uncles next Christmas, or simply to satisfy that inner thirst to be Thurston.

EAT

BRITTO'S
International, Goan $$

⏱ **8am-late**

Long-running, usually packed-to-the-gills, and sometimes open as late as 3am, Britto's glorified beach shack tumbles out onto the beach, serving up a healthy mixture of Goan and Continental cuisines (try the fiery pork *vindaho* for a truly local treat), satisfying cakes and delicious desserts, all accompanied by the strains (or the straining) of live music or karaoke several nights a week.

J&A'S *Italian* $$$
☎ **3139488; www.littleitalygoa.com;**
⏱ **lunch & dinner**

A pretty cafe set around a gorgeous little Portuguese villa, this little slice of Italy is a treat even before the sumptuous food arrives. Owned by a wonderful couple originally from Mumbai, the jazz-infused garden with twinkling evening lights makes for a place as drenched in romance as a tiramisu is in rum. Add to this triple-filtered water, an electric

car, and composted leftovers, and you've got an experience almost as good for the world as it is for your tastebuds.

LE POISSON ROUGE
Mediterranean $$$
☎ **3245800;** ⏱ **7pm-late**

Baga manages to produce fine dining with finesse, and this French-slanted experience is one of the picks of the place. Simple local ingredients are combined into winning dishes such as beetroot carpaccio and red-snapper masala, and served up beneath the stars.

LILA CAFÉ
International, Bakery $$
⏱ **8.30am-6pm Wed-Mon**

Airy, white and enticing is this roomy semi–open air place along the river, run by long-term German expats and with a great line in home-baked breads and perfect, frothy cappuccinos. The restful river view is somewhat obscured by the cafe's own guest-parking places, but it still makes for a soothing place for a quiet cuppa.

DRINK

CAVALA SEASIDE RESORT
Hotel Bar
☎ **2276090; www.cavala.com**

Idiosyncratic, ivy-clad Cavala hotel has been charming Baga-bound travellers for more than 25 years, and its bar, complete with frequent live music and weekly karaoke, cooks up a storm most evenings.

ⓨ MUBLI CYBERCAFE
Internet Cafe

Tito's Rd; ☻ **9am-late**

Sip an Italian coffee and check your emails at this friendly 1st-floor place hidden away from the Tito's Rd action.

★ PLAY

✿ CAFÉ MAMBO *Club*

☎ **9822765002; www.titos.in; before/ after 10pm free/Rs 200;** ☻ **8pm-late**

Owned and managed by Tito's (below), this is a – very slightly – more sophisticated version of the same thing, with nightly DJs pumping out commercial house, hip hop and Latino tunes.

✿ ON THE ROCKS *Club*

☎ **2277879;** ☻ **8pm-late**

Further down towards Baga Beach from Tito's, On the Rocks offers a slicker, more stylish alternative to the mayhem found at the maraud-ing mammoth up the road.

✿ TITO'S *Club*

☎ **9822765002; www.titos.in; men/ women from Rs 300/free;** ☻ **8pm-3am**

Tito's, the titan on Goa's club-bing scene, is trying its hardest to escape the locals-leering-

at-Western-women image of yesteryear, though it's still hardly the place for a hassle-free girls' night out. Thursday's Bollywood Night and Friday's hip hop are the pick of the bunch, for the closest thing to the Canaries this side of Star TV.

Beef up your Bollywood moves at Tito's

>CANDOLIM & SINQUERIM

Candolim's long, narrow beach, which curves round to join smaller Sinquerim to the south, is largely the preserve of slow-basting package tourists from the UK, Russia and Scandinavia, and is fringed with an un-abating line of beach shacks, all offering sunbeds and shade in exchange for your custom.

By far the most bewildering thing here, however, is the hulking wreck of the *River Princess* tanker, which ran aground in the late 1990s. Nothing can quite prepare you for the surreal sight of this massive industrial creature, marooned just a few dozen metres offshore, with tourists sun-bathing in her sullen shadow.

Back from the beach, bustling Fort Aguada Rd is the best place to head for shops, services, and for perusing the dozens of restaurants which awaken each evening to provide cocktails, dinners of different culinary persuasions, and the odd spot of live music. The beach, meanwhile, is Candolim's other option for night life, where the shacks host happy hours and jam sessions well beyond sunset.

CANDOLIM & SINQUERIM

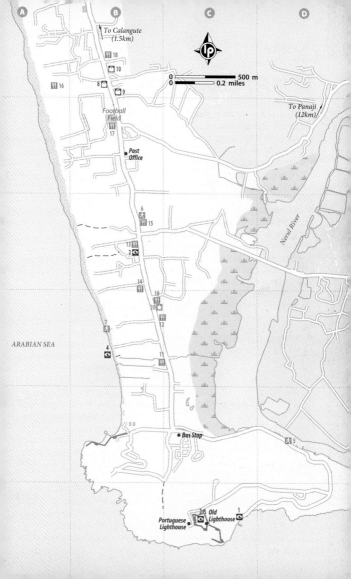

To Calangute
(1.5km)

0   500 m
0   0.2 miles

To Panaji
(12km)

Football
Field

Post
Office

ARABIAN SEA

Nerul River

Bus Stop

Portuguese
Lighthouse

Old
Lighthouse

◉ SEE

◎ AGUADA JAIL

Gazing out melancholically to the broad Mandovi River is Fort Aguada jail, Goa's largest prison, whose cells stand on the site that once formed the citadel of the hilltop fort (see right) above. Today the prison mostly houses inmates serving sentences for drug possession or smuggling, including a dozen or so long-staying foreigners. The road down to the jail's entrance – which is as far, thankfully, as most people ever get – passes a weird and wonderful compound known as Jimmy's Palace, home to reclusive tycoon, Jimmy Gazdar. Designed by Goan architect Gerard de Cunha, it's a

GOA SUPREME

Fans of the enigmatic Jason Bourne might recognise a small road bridge, spanning the Nerul River north of Candolim, from which Bourne's girlfriend plunged to a watery grave following a high-octane *Bourne Supremacy* (2004) car chase.

This scene was one of several filmed in Goa, with the film hopping from Palolem (p110) to Panaji (p78) and on to Candolim. But if you really want to tread in Bourne's footsteps, check in – as did his alter ego, Matt Damon – into the nearby Fort Aguada Beach Resort (p124) to see how the amnesiac assassin kicked back after a long, hot day of filming.

closely guarded froth of fountains, foliage and follies, of which you'll catch glimpses as you whiz past.

◎ CALIZZ

☎ 325000; www.calizz.com; Fort Aguada Rd; Admission Rs 300; ⏰ 10am-7pm
A highlight of Candolim for anyone even faintly interested in Goan heritage is this impressive compound filled with traditional, transplanted Goan houses, complete with authentic interiors. Tours, which last for 45 minutes, are conducted by historians to bring the state's cultural history to life, in this National Tourism Award–winning project.

◎ FORT AGUADA

Constructed by the Portuguese in 1612 to guard the mouth of the Mandovi estuary, this is without doubt the most impressive and imposing of Goa's remaining forts. It's worth braving the crowds of domestic tourists and attendant hawkers for the views from the moated ruins on the hilltop, beside the still functioning four-storey Portuguese lighthouse, built in 1894 – the oldest of its type in Asia.

◎ THE RIVER PRINCESS

An eyesore or an engaging oddity, depending on your point of view, this rusty run-aground princess has been blighting (or gracing)

Candolim's beachfront for years, and though plans to haul her off often surface, they never quite seem to come to fruition. If you're an adventurous sort, there's little to stop you swimming or wading out to the ship and climbing the rope ladder; land-lubbers might prefer to admire her from more of a distance.

DO

EXCURSION-BOAT JETTY
Daytrips

If you're looking to haggle for an on-the-spot dolphin-spotting trip, head up to this jetty on the banks of the Nerul River, from which lots of independent local boatmen op-

erate and sell their services mostly to a domestic-holidaying crowd.

JOHN'S BOAT TOURS
Daytrips

☎ 5620190, 9822182814; www.digital goa.com/johnsboattours; Fort Aguada Rd; houseboat cruises per person per day Rs 4300

One of the most organised of Candolim's daytripping options, John's has been offering a variety of boat and jeep excursions for years, as well as arranging fabulous, river-based houseboat cruises. A dolphin-watching trip costs Rs 795; a boat trip to Anjuna Market and back goes for Rs 500, and a 'Crocodile Dundee' river trip,

The River Princess, marooned just off Candolim Beach, is an intriguing sight

All aboard: dolphin-watching cruise (p71), Candolim

SHOP

FABINDIA *Lifestyle Store*
Seashell Arcade, Fort Aguada Rd;
10.30am-9pm
Part of a nationwide chain selling tempting fair-trade bed and table linens, home furnishings, clothes, jewellery and toiletries, this makes for a great, colourful browse, perfect for picking up high-end gifts or treating yourself to a traditional *kurta* (shirt) or *salwar kameez* (a long dresslike tunic worn over baggy trousers) outfit.

NEWTON'S *Groceries*
Fort Aguada Rd; 9.30am-midnight
If you're desperately missing Edam cheese or Pot Noodles, don't delay in dashing to Newton's, to stock up satisfyingly homely goods of all descriptions. This vast supermarket also stocks a good line in toiletries, wines and children's toys, and expat folks travel miles just to peruse its goodies-lined shelves.

SOTOHAUS *Lifestyle Store*
2489983; www.sotodecor.com;
Fort Aguada Rd
Offering cool, functional items dreamed up by a Swiss expat team, this is the place to invest in a natural form–inspired lamp, mirror or dining table, to add a twist of streamlined India to your pad back home.

to catch a glimpse of the Mandovi's crocodile 'muggers', costs Rs 1000 per person.

WATER SPORTS *Water Sports*
The southern stretch of Candolim Beach, and Sinquerim Beach beyond it, are home to plenty of independent water-sports operators, who offer jet skis, parasailing, waterskiing and the usual host of watery activities. Haggle hard to get the very best rate.

¶ Nazneen Sarosh-Rebelo
Co-owner of Café Chocolatti (p74) and passionate chocolate maker

How long have you been living here in Candolim? I've been here for 15 years; I grew up in England, and met my husband, who's Goan, here on holiday. This is the cafe's sixth season. **Why chocolate?** I'm a speech and language therapist, but have always had a passion for cooking and experimented with chocolates at home. Gradually, friends started buying the chocolates I was making, and I opened a little shop, which slowly became the cafe. **What are your culinary highlights of Goa?** Definitely the fish and seafood, especially if it's prepared simply, because I think the flavours can be drowned in too many masalas. A snapper, perhaps, is perfect, in garlic and olive oil. **And your favourite chocolate creations?** I love the challenge of introducing something new: hand-rolled truffles or marmalade chocolate brownies. And ginger cake; it reminds me of England.

BEACHES & TOWNS

CANDOLIM & SINQUERIM

EAT

¶ BANYAN TREE
Southeast Asian $$$

☎ 664 5858; Taj Holiday Village,
Fort Aguada Rd; ⏲ 7.30-10.30pm
Refined Thai food is the trademark
of the Taj's romantic Banyan Tree,
its swish courtyard set beneath
the branches of a vast old banyan
tree. If you're a fan of green curry,
don't, whatever you do, miss the
succulent, signature version on
offer here.

¶ BOMRA'S *Southeast Asian* $$
Fort Aguada Rd
Fabulously unusual cuisine is
on offer at this sleek little place,
tucked into a courtyard just next
door to Candolim's Butter night-
club (opposite; look for the huge
golden saxophone), and serving
interesting Burmese cuisine with
a fusion twist. Try it once, and
you'll undoubtedly be back for
more.

¶ CAFÉ CHOCOLATTI
Mediterranean $$
Fort Aguada Rd; ⏲ 9am-7pm
Treat yourself to serene sanctu-
ary at this lovely tearoom, set in a
green garden light years from the
bustle of the beach. Though the
cafe also serves sandwiches and
salads (the pear, rocket and blue
cheese combination is divine), the
clue to its speciality is in the name.

Order a ginger-lime fizz and a slice
of double chocolate cake and sink
back into cocoa heaven.

¶ CINNABAR *Snacks, Drinks* $$
Acron Arcade, Fort Aguada Rd
This corner joint set in the Acron
Arcade shopping centre makes for
a calming pit stop on the shady
terrace. Snack from an uncompli-
cated bistro menu of pastas, soups
and salads, then top it off with a
Black Forest ice cream and a frothy
coffee.

¶ L'ORANGE *Mediterranean* $$
Fort Aguada Rd; ⏲ noon-midnight
A cute, and largely orange restau-
rant, bar and art gallery just beside
John's Boat Tours; head here on
Tuesday and Thursday nights for
'live music by Elvis', who's appar-
ently alive and well and living in
Candolim.

¶ PETE'S SHACK
Beach Shack $$
Amid an ocean of beach shacks
(with such notables as Peter
Stringfellow, Jim Morrison and Bob
Marley vying for business along-
side Pete), Pete's stands out at the
northern end of the strip as one of
the sleekest, coolest beachfront
operations. Good tunes, tasty sal-
ads, and scrumptious desserts keep
the holidaying crowds coming
back for more.

🍴 REPUBLIC OF NOODLES
Southeast Asian $$$

Fort Aguada Rd; ⏲ **11.30am-3pm, 7-11pm**

For a sophisticated dining experience, the RoN delivers with its dark bamboo interior, Buddha heads and floating candles. Huge noodle plates are the order of the day, and if you're feeling flush there's an exquisite brunch on Sunday mornings: Rs 1200 buys you an extensive Southeast Asian buffet, along with unlimited Mimosas and Bloody Marys to pep up your weekend.

🍴 SAI'S VIVA GOA!
Seafood, Goan $

Fort Aguada Rd; ⏲ **11am-midnight**

This cheap, locals-oriented little place serves flipping-fresh fish and Goan seafood specialities such as a spicy mussel fry, also popular with adventurous foreigners who long to stray from the usual beachside fare.

🍴 STONE HOUSE
International $$

Fort Aguada Rd; ⏲ **6pm-midnight**

Surf 'n' turf's the thing at this venerable old Candolim venue, which inhabits a stone house with a leafy front courtyard, and the improbable sounding 'Swedish Lobster' tops the list. There's live music most nights of the week, amid the twinkle of fairy lights.

Republic of Noodles' ambient dining space

⭐ PLAY

🎴 BUTTER *Bar, Club*

Fort Aguada Rd; ⏲ **7pm-late**

A golden saxophone marks the entrance to the huge Butter lounge-bar complex, which gears up nightly, hosting international guest DJs and the annual Sunburn Festival (see p24).

>PANAJI & THE CENTRAL COAST

Goa's central coastline might not be packed with beautiful beaches, but what it lacks in sands it makes up for with a wealth of historic and natural riches, tightly packed in between the Mandovi and Zuari Rivers. This is the place to see the 'authentic' face of Goa, and get a sense of what the state felt like before the tourists moved in.

Panaji (also known as Panjim), state capital since 1843, is an easy, breezy city, compact enough to wander without the need for public transport. Meanwhile Old Goa, east along the river, is at once an impressive reminder of the might of the medieval Catholic Church, and a forlorn example of how a grand city can fall.

But what's best is that all the cultural and bucolic charms of central Goa can easily be reached from any beach destination along the coast, meaning you won't have to forsake your favourite beachside spot for more than just a few pleasurable, culture-rich hours.

PANAJI & THE CENTRAL COAST

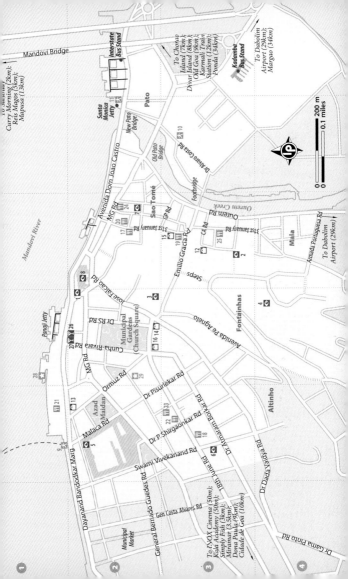

PANAJI

SEE

◉ ABBÉ FARIA STATUE
Avenida Dom Joao Castro
What looks like a scene from a *Hammer House of Horror* hit is actually a statuesque testament to one of Goa's most famous exports, 18th-century Candolim-born Abbé Faria, a cleric who became a close confidante of Napoleon's and who was one of the forefathers of modern hypnotism. Here he's displayed in full dramatic throes, 'pouncing', as Graham Greene once noted, 'like a great black eagle on his mesmerised female patient'.

HYPNOSIS!
Abbé Faria, born the humble son of a monk and a nun in Candolim in 1756, is one of history's enigmatic figures, having hovered on the sidelines of the greatest events of the 18th century and flirted with its main players (Robespierre and Napoleon being just two of them), whilst remaining an elusive outsider, caught in a world of black magic and esoteric pursuits. He is considered the 'father of modern hypnotism' for his explanations on the power of suggestion – unchartered territory at the time. Next time you see a stage hypnotist parading the tricks of the trade, watch too for the ghost of Custodio Faria, flitting restively in the wings.

◉ CHAPEL OF ST SEBASTIAN
St Sebastian Rd
This pretty little chapel, built in 1818, is home to an unusual open-eyed crucifix, which was originally designed to terrify those accused of heretical crimes at Old Goa's notorious Palace of the Inquisition. More cheerfully, the chapel also hosts an annual celebration and street fair to mark the Feast of Our Lady of Livrament in mid-November.

◉ CHURCH OF OUR LADY OF THE IMMACULATE CONCEPTION
Stacked lavishly high above the municipal gardens, Panaji's centrepiece is this gorgeous 17th-century church, as gold-plated, floral and multicoloured on the inside as it is gleaming white and wedding cake–like on the out. This is where old-time sailors arrived to thank their lucky stars – and saints – after a successful sailing from Lisbon, and where a street fair spills forth each December to mark the festival of Our Lady.

◉ FONTAINHAS & SAO TOMÉ
Panaji's atmospheric old Portuguese quarters, squeezed between Ourem Creek and Altinho Hill and centring on 31st January Rd, make for a lovely stroll: admire the overhanging balconies, narrow streets, colour-washed

buildings and congenial small-town atmosphere. Pop into a local chai shop for a quick tea stop, or a hole-in-the-wall bar for a stronger, frothier pick-me-up and a dose of local conversation.

◎ INSTITUTE MENENEZ BRAGANZA
Malaca Rd; ⏱ 9.30am-1.15pm & 2-5.45pm Mon-Fri
Step into the west entrance of the town's public library, to examine the grand and dramatic *azulejos* (traditional painted ceramic tiles) adorning the wall, which

depict scenes from *Os Lusiadas,* a famously epic and glorious Portuguese poem that tells the tale of Portugal's 15th- and 16th-century voyages of discovery.

◎ PUBLIC OBSERVATORY
Swami Vivekanand Rd; ⏱ 7-9pm Nov-May
Five telescopes reach for the stars at Panaji's public observatory, located on the terrace of Junta House, where the city's Association of Friends of Astronomy skilfully searches the skies.

Feel the magic of Panaji's Abbé Faria statue

BEACHES & TOWNS

PANAJI & THE CENTRAL COAST

✪ SECRETARIAT BUILDING
Avenida Dom Joao Castro
Goa's oldest colonial building, this was once the moated palace of 15th-century Muslim sultan Yussuf Adil Shah who controlled Goa before the Portuguese took a fancy to both the state and his home in 1510. It now houses dry-as-dust governmental buildings and is currently undergoing extensive renovations.

DO
🏃 FERRY TO BETIM *Ferry*
Dayanand Bandodkar Marg;
⏱ every 20 min 6am-10pm
If you're in the mood for something less slick than a full-blown cruise, hop aboard the overloaded ferry across the Mandovi to Betim, shoulder to shoulder with scores of bustling locals. Though there's nothing much to do when you get there except to turn around and head back again, it's worth it for the riverine view of Panaji and the workaday atmosphere.

🏃 GOA TOURISM DEVELOPMENT COMPANY DAYTRIPS *Daytrip*
☎ 2424001; www.goa-tourism.com; Dr Alvares Costa Rd; ⏱ 9.30am-5.45pm Mon-Fri
If you want to get out and about in the Goan hinterland without

your own set of wheels, hop aboard a whirlwind GTDC tour, which sends air-conditioned buses from Panaji hurtling all across the state. Check out the website to see what's on offer, or book tours at Panaji's GTDC office.

🏃 SATURDAY CURRY MORNING *Courses*
www.holidayonthemenu.com; Betim; curry morning £59; ⏱ 9.30am-2pm Sat
Delicious cooking courses are run from a purpose-built kitchen just across the river at Betim, and the Saturday Curry Morning, which runs from 9.30am to 2pm, is just the thing for those not wanting to spend a whole week chopping and grinding. Courses must be booked in advance, after which you'll receive details of how to get to the aromatic Indian kitchen.

🏃 SUNSET BOAT CRUISE *Daytrips*
Santa Monica Jetty; cruises per person Rs 150; ⏱ GTDC sunset cruise 6pm & 6.30pm, GTDC sundown cruise 7.15pm & 7.45pm
A host of floats sets out each evening just before sunset to ply the Mandovi waters and entertain tourists with nothing more sophisticated than the view, a beer or two and a dash of traditional Goan dancing. A number of companies run competing tours

rom the Santa Monica Jetty, with the GTDC's being the most serene and least raucous of the bunch. Head to the jetty to compare watery offerings and pick up your tickets.

SHOP

BOMBAY STORES
Lifestyle Store

☎ 2230333; St Sebastian Rd

Selling high-quality gifts, crafts, textiles, beauty products, tea and jewellery, Bombay Stores makes for good gift shopping, with the slightly befuddling slogan 'Treasures to Gift, Gifts to Treasure'.

FUSION ACCESS
Lifestyle Store

☎ 6650342; www.fusionaccess.com; 13/32 Ormuz Rd

A cool 1st-floor treasure trove, filled with beautiful reproduction antiques – from beds to bedside lamps – textiles, richly illustrated books on Goa, and lots of other enticing goodies.

SINGBAL'S BOOK HOUSE
Books

☎ 2425747; Church Sq; ⏰ 9.30am-1pm & 3.30-7.30pm Mon-Sat

A wide selection of international magazines and newspapers, and lots of books on Goa, is offered at this slightly grumpy but well-stocked establishment right on the edge of the municipal gardens.

SOSA'S *Clothes*

☎ 2228063; E245 Ourem Rd

A chic boutique carrying local labels such as Horn Ok Please, Hidden Harmony and Free Falling, Sosa's is the best place in Panaji to source upscale Indian fashion.

VISIONWORLD BOOK DEPOT *Books*

☎ 2182865; Church Sq; ⏰ 9.30am-9pm

Offering up a good selection of self-help and spiritual titles, novels and children's books, the ladies of this nice little place also vend an assortment of locally made snacks to provide sustenance for your Panaji wanderings.

EAT

ANANDASHRAM
Goan, Indian $

⏰ noon-3.15pm & 7.30-10.30pm

Just opposite the Hospedaria Venite (see p82), this little place dishes up simple, mighty tasty fish curries and veg and nonveg thalis for around the Rs 40 mark.

GUJARAT SWEET MART
Snacks, Drinks $

Gujarat Lodge, 18th June Rd

If you possessed a single sweet tooth, here's the place to indulge it, with a pantheon of Indian

BEACHES & TOWNS

PANAJI & THE CENTRAL COAST

BEST BREAKFAST BITES

Start your day the local way, by ordering a glass of sweet chai and one of the following South Indian breakfast classics, all widely available wherever you see hungry locals heading soon after sunrise:

> *Bhaji pau* – fresh bread rolls dunked in a small curry side dish
> *Masala dosa* – a paper-thin rice pancake stuffed with spiced potato and onion
> *Idli sambar* – Steamed rice cakes served with a thin souplike lentil sauce
> *Puri bhaji* – puffed-up deep-fried bread served with a spicy curry side dish
> *Onion uttapam* – griddle-fried, crumpetlike rice pancake, flecked with fried onions

confectionaries of the sweet, sweeter and sweetest varieties. Wash all that decadence down with a thick milkshake or lassi, both of which come in an array of heavenly, sugary flavours.

🍴 HORSE SHOE
Goan, International $$

☎ 2431788; Ourem Rd; ⏱ 7-10.30pm
A well-respected, sweet little Goan-Portuguese place, this is a simple but romantic choice for some traditional dishes and a nice bottle of Portuguese wine. At the time of research Horse Shoe was open for dinner only but this might change, so call ahead to be sure.

🍴 HOSPEDARIA VENITE
Goan, Seafood $$

31st January Rd
Along with Viva Panjim (opposite), this is the lunch address to which most tourists head and, though the food isn't excellent, the atmos-

phere warrants the visit. Its tiny, rickety balcony tables, looking out onto pastel-washed 31st January Rd, make the perfect lunchtime spot, and the Goan *chouriços* (spiced sausages) and vegetable *vindalho* (fiery Goan curry) are actually pretty tasty. Order a cold beer or two, munch on a slightly '70s-style salad (think cold boiled vegetables in vinaigrette) and watch lazy Panaji slip by.

🍴 QUARTERDECK
International $$

Dayanand Bandodkar Marg
Watch crammed passenger ferries and hulking casino boats chug by from a waterside table at this open-air 'multicuisine' restaurant perched on the banks of the Mandovi. There's a small playground for children and the multicuisine is tasty enough, though the location is without doubt the restaurant's biggest drawcard.

SHER-E-PUNJAB *Indian* $$
8th June Rd
A cut above the usual lunch point, Sher-E-Punjab caters to well-dressed locals with its generous, carefully spiced Indian dishes. There's a pleasant garden terrace out back, and an icy air-conditioned room if you're feeling sticky. Don't miss the delicious *tandoori paneer tikka* (Indian cheese with mustardy tandoori spices), but note, if you're hungering for snacks, the fish fingers and chicken fingers are 'seasonal only'.

VEG BABA *Indian, Vegetarian* $
Eagle Vision Bldg, off 18th June Rd
This spanking new place down a side street off 18th June Rd dishes up delicious Indian vegetarian delights of all descriptions, and friendly, cheerful and efficient. A self-declared 'meat-free zone', it's clean, cool and blessed with a good line in proverbs: 'An elephant is 50 times stronger,' it reminds us sagely, 'it is vegetarian.'

VIHAR RESTAURANT *Indian, Vegetarian* $
G Rd
A vast menu of 'pure-veg' food, great big thalis (metal lunch plates, piled up with the 'bit of everything' approach) and a plethora of fresh juices make this clean, simple canteen a popular place for locals and visitors alike. Sip a hot chai, invent your own juice combination and dig into an ice cream for afters.

VIVA PANJIM *Goan, Indian* $$
31st January Rd; 11.30am-3pm & 7-11pm Mon-Sat, 7-11pm Sun
Though it might be more than a touch touristy these days, this little side-street eatery, with a couple of tables out on the street itself, still delivers tasty Goan staples, as well as a standard line in Indian fare. Keep an eye out in the dim interior for Mrs Linda de Souza, restaurant founder and doughty matriarch.

DRINK
CASA MENENEZ BAR *Local Bar*
Dayanand Bandodkar Marg; 11am-3pm & 7-10.30pm
One of dozens of down-to-earth drinking holes scattered along the river road and around the municipal gardens, this friendly place, open to the street and with just a scattering of plastic tables, is great for grabbing a cool Kingfisher.

TOP GEAR PUB *Local Bar*
Dayanand Bandodkar Marg; 11am-3pm & 6.30pm-midnight
A few doors down from Casa Menenez (above), there's a tiny, cool, retro bar hidden behind Top

Gear's unassuming doors. There's no food here, so don't come hungry, but it's a great place to wet your whistle or whet your appetite.

PLAY

☆ CASINO ROYALE Casino
☎ 6659400; www.casinoroyalegoa.com; Dayanand Bandodkar Marg; admission Mon-Thu Rs 1500, Fri-Sun Rs 1800
⏱ 6pm-8am

The newest and largest of Goa's floating casinos, this upscale floating shrine to all things speculative will have you losing your money all night long. Various age and dress restrictions apply; call to book your slot at the slots.

☆ CINE NACIONAL Cinema
Ormuz Rd; tickets Rs 50

If you're up for a bit of grim local grime, you've found the place at the Nacional. It's dismal, dark and dank, but with unique appeal if you're looking for an unforgettable dose of Bollywood. Just make sure you don't drink too much Coke, as the only filmic quality the toilets possess is their likeness to a certain scene in *Trainspotting*. Films are shown around four times daily; check at the box office for current screenings.

☆ INOX CINEMA Cinema
☎ 2420999; www.inoxmovies.com; Old GMC Heritage Precinct

This comfortable, plush multiplex cinema, which shows Hollywood and Bollywood blockbusters alike is near the Kala Academy (below). If you have internet access, you can even try your hand at online booking and choose your seats in advance.

☆ KALA ACADEMY Music, Dance
☎ 2420451; www.kalaacademy.org; Dayanand Bandodkar Marg

On the west side of the city at Campal is Goa's premier cultural centre, which features a program of dance, theatre, music and art exhibitions throughout the year. Many shows are in Konkani, but there are occasional English-language productions; call to find out what's on when you're in town.

REIS MAGOS

SEE

◉ REIS MAGOS CHURCH
⏱ 9am-noon & 4-5.30pm Mon-Sat, Sun for services

Built in 1555, probably on the site of an old Hindu temple, this church acts as the eternal home to several Portuguese viceroys, as well as Dom Luis de Atade who, for 10 months in 1570, kept an invading Muslim army of 100,000 men and 2000 elephants at bay with his own force of just 7000. Today, though, the church is most famous for its Reis Magos (Wise Men) Festival on 6 January, which sees a re-enactment of the arrival of the three wise men, complete with gifts for the infant Jesus.

 REIS MAGOS FORT

Like Fort Aguada (p70) further up the coast, modern Goans have paid homage to the strength of Portuguese fort-building in their own special way: by locking up present-day prisoners within the structure originally designed to keep the naughty folk out. Though the 1551 Reis Magos fort is out of bounds to law-abiding citizens, it makes an imposing sight – from a safe distance.

The village of Reis Magos, containing both church and fort, is northwest of Panaji, about 5km by road; to reach here, take a taxi or a bus headed from Panaji, via Betim, to Candolim, and ask to be dropped off at Reis Magos.

MIRAMAR

 SEE

CABO RAJ BHAVAN

www.rajbhavangoa.org; 🕙 chapel Sunday mass 9.30-10.30am

What's now the official residence of the governor of Goa was once

Entrance to the Old British Cemetery at Cabo Raj Bhavan

a Portuguese fort, built in the 17th century to guard the mouth of the Mandovi and Zuari Rivers, and situated around 1km south of Miramar Beach. From 1799 to 1813, the site – along with several other forts in Goa – was briefly occupied by British troops, attested to by the small British cemetery, which was later used for rice cultivation, and its gravestones for sharpening scythes. Today it makes for a fascinating wander, along with a peek into Raj Bhavan's 500-year-old chapel that holds its Feast of the Chapel each 15 August, which draws thousands of locals for prayers and festivities.

⦿ MIRAMAR BEACH

Compared with most of Goa's beaches, long, wide Miramar – popular with out-of-state daytrippers – is certainly nothing special, but its south end is an interesting locally flavoured place to catch the sunset among the fishing boats on your way home from a daytrip to Panaji. At the northern end of the beach you'll find Gaspar Dias, which was once the site of a fort built to match the still-standing Reis Magos Fort (p85) on the other side of the Mandovi River. Gracing the spot today stands a statue representing Goa's famed Hindu–Christian unity.

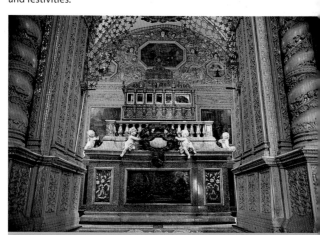
The mausoleum of Goa's patron saint, St Francis Xavier, lies in old Goa's Basilica of Bom Jesus (p88)

EAT

SIMPLY FISH

International, Seafood $$$

☎ 2463333; Goa Marriott; 🕒 dinner

The restaurants and bars of this upscale five-star hotel, which clings to the sands of Miramar Beach, are some of the favourites of well-heeled Panjimites looking to treat themselves. Simply Fish, of all the restaurants on offer, is the one to plump for, offering up such exotic fishy delights as lobster cappuccino and mud-crab *xacuti* (a spicy chicken or meat dish with coconut milk). Otherwise, lunch or even just a drink at the all-day Waterfront Terrace and Bar is a more simple, similarly soothing pleasure.

DONA PAULA

 ## SEE

DONA PAULA BEACH

Situated 9km southwest of Panaji, on the headland that divides the Zuari and Mandovi Rivers, Dona Paula allegedly took its name from Dona Paula de Menenez, a Portuguese viceroy's daughter who threw herself from the clifftop to Davy Jones' locker after being prevented from marrying a local fisherman. Her tombstone, which attests to her grizzly fate, still stands in the chapel at the Cabo Raj Bhavan (p85). Though the views out over Miramar Beach and Mormugao Bay are nice enough, the drab village and persistent hawkers could, given enough time, inspire you to consider a fate similar to the dear Dona.

IMAGES OF INDIA STATUE

For the last 40 years, Baroness Yrsa von Leistner's (1917–2008) whitewashed *Images of India* statue has graced Dona Paula's sea front, portraying a couple looking off in different directions; the man towards India's past and the woman towards the future. 'Ain't it always the way?

EAT

CIDADE DE GOA

International $$$

☎ 2454545; www.cidadedegoa.com

After a day of poking about the coastline, a good place to recover before heading homeward is at one of the eight restaurants at this swanky village-style place, designed by renowned Goan architect Charles Correa, close to Dona Paula in the village of Vainguinim. Chow down at its Portuguese-themed Alfama restaurant, which comes complete with wandering minstrels, or just drop in for a cool sundowner at the Bar Latino.

WORTH THE TRIP

Though it might be hard to imagine today, World Heritage–listed Old Goa was once the 'Rome of the East', a mighty Catholic metropolis eclipsing everything ever seen before in the vast Asian continent. Over the centuries, however, outbreaks of malaria and cholera in this ecclesiastical oasis amid the marshes eventually led to the city's abandonment, leaving Old Goa to just a few ghosts and grim hangers-on. Old Goa, these days, is a stately monument to empires past, and to the flawed dreams of its conquerors. Buses make the 20-minute journey to Old Goa regularly from Panaji, while a taxi from the state capital will whisk you here in even less time. All churches are open from early morning to well beyond sunset, and admission is free.

No trip to Old Goa would be complete without a visit to the **Basilica of Bom Jesus**. Famous throughout the Roman Catholic world for its rather grizzled and grizzly long-term resident, the basilica's vast, gilded interior forms the last resting place of Goa's patron saint, St Francis Xavier who, in 1541, embarked on a mission to put right the sinful, heady lifestyles of Goa's Portuguese colonials. St Francis himself is these days housed in a mausoleum to the right, in a glass-sided coffin amid a shower of gilt stars.

On the opposite side of the central square, the **Church of St Francis of Assisi** is a beautifully fading structure built in 1661 over an earlier 16th-century chapel. The lovely interior is filled with gilded and carved woodwork, murals depicting the life of St Francis, and 16th-century Portuguese tombstones. Note the sign inside that reads 'No Photography of Persons'. Presumably, they've no problem with you clicking pictures of any heavenly hosts that decide to put in an appearance.

Nearby, the melancholy, evocative ruins of the **Monastery of St Augustine** are all that remain of a huge structure founded in 1572 and finally abandoned in 1835. The building's facade, once vast and impressive, came tumbling down in 1942; all that remains, among piles of rubble, is the towering skeletal belfry.

Finally, whilst in Old Goa, don't miss a peek into the **Sé Cathedral**, or Sé de Santa Catarina, as it's known by its full name, the largest church in Asia, on which building commenced in 1562 and finally wrapped up in 1652. In the belfry sits its Golden Bell, the largest bell in Asia, while indoors you'll find a little screened chapel known as the Chapel of the Cross of Miracles, wherein sits a cross said to have miraculously expanded in size after its creation in 1619.

Following your explorations of Old Goa, venture to nearby **Divar Island**, a picturesque island filled with crumbling Portuguese homes and colourful scenes from traditional Goan life. Hop aboard a **ferry** (pedestrian/motorbike/car free/Rs 4/20; ☼ every 30min 6am-2am) from Old Goa to explore the island's quiet byways and peaceful largest village, Piedade.

Alternatively, head to the **Dr Salim Ali Bird Sanctuary**, a mangrove-laden reserve on the island of Chorao, which features such avian treasures as herons, kingfishers, drongos and mynah birds. To get here, cross the river by **ferry** (pedestrian/motorbike/car free/Rs 4/20; ☼ every 30min 6.30am-9pm) from Ribander, between Old Goa and Panaji, then negotiate a rate for a sanctuary **tour** (around Rs 400, sanctuary entry Rs 50) by canoe, at the ferry landing.

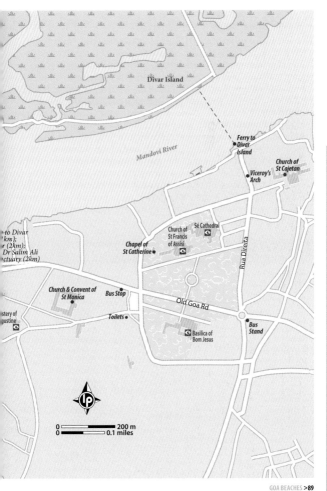

Divar Island

Mandovi River

Ferry to Divar Island

Church of St Cajetan

Viceroy's Arch

Sé Cathedral

Church of St Francis of Assisi

Chapel of St Catherine

Rua Direita

to Divar km); r (2km); Dr Salim Ali ctuary (2km)

Church & Convent of St Monica

Bus Stop

Old Goa Rd

stery of ustine

Toilets

Bus Stand

Basilica of Bom Jesus

0 ———— 200 m
0 ———— 0.1 miles

>COLVA, BENAULIM & AROUND

The northern portion of south Goa's coastline extends from Bogmalo, just a few kilometres from Dabolim airport (Map p91, A1), down to Mobor, perched on the headland above the mouth of the Sal River. The main resorts here are Colva and Benaulim, both rather lacklustre compared with the smaller villages that dot the coastal road, but nevertheless equipped with decent facilities and a range of restaurants. Colva, in particular, tends to attract a domestic-holidaying crowd, whilst Benaulim is a lower-budget, marginally more atmospheric choice. Meanwhile, Cavelossim, further south, is a firm favourite on package-holiday itineraries, with a scruffy village, a quietly buzzing nightlife and a long, uninterrupted beach.

To experience the beauty of this area, however, head to the deserted stretches of beach between the main resorts, where you'll find little except sea birds floating on the thermals and scuttling sand crabs to keep you company. Rent a scooter for a day or two to buzz along the gentle coastal lanes, past dozens of *palaços* (palaces), wallowing water buffalo and bustling village life.

COLVA, BENAULIM & AROUND

◉ SEE
Arossim Beach	1	B1
Betelbatim Beach	2	B2
Bogmalo Beach	3	A1
Cavelossim Beach	4	C5
Majorda Beach	5	B2
Mobor Beach	6	C6
Naval Aviation Museum	7	A1
Old Anchor Hotel	8	C5
Our Lady of Remedious Chapel	9	B1
Utorda Beach	10	B2
Varca Beach	11	C4
Velsao Beach	12	B1

🏃 DO
Betty's Place Boat Trips	13	C5
Boat Tours & Water Sports	14	A1
Boat Trips	15	B2
Ferry to Assolna	16	D5
Goa Diving	17	A1
Horse Riding	(see 25)	
Sereno Spa	(see 22)	
Treat Yourself Health Centre	18	B2

🛍 SHOP
Saga	19	C5
Treasure	20	B1

🍴 EAT
Blue Whale	21	C6
Casa Sarita	22	B2
Coconut Creek	23	A1
Full Moon Café	24	A1
Greenland Bar & Restaurant	25	B2
Leela Kempinski	26	C6
Mallika	27	B2
Martin's Corner	28	B2
Papa Joe's	29	C5
Raj's Pentagon Restaurant & Garden Pub	30	B2
Rice Bowl	31	C5
Zeebop by the Sea	32	B2

⭐ PLAY
Jazz Inn	33	C5

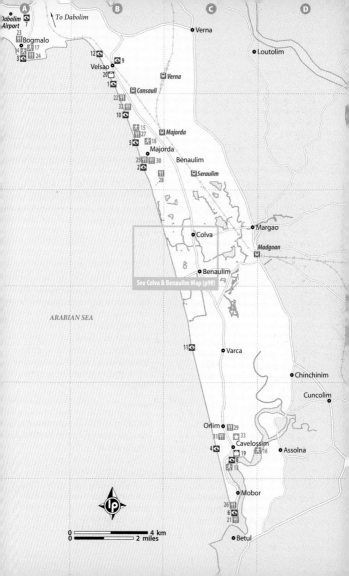

BOGMALO

SEE

◉ BOGMALO BEACH

Map p91

A small and once picturesque bay, now within roaring distance of Dabolim airport, this small stretch of sand makes a decent stop if you've got an hour or two to kill before a flight, or if you're keen to experience Goa's underwater scene, courtesy of its highly respected diving outlet. Otherwise, it's not especially appealing, cramped with ragtag stalls, beach cafes and spluttering busloads of excitable domestic daytrippers.

◉ NAVAL AVIATION MUSEUM

Map p91; ☎ 5995525; adult/child Rs 20/5; ⏱ 10am-5pm Sun-Tue

If you've exhausted your options or your patience for hawkers down on Bogmalo Beach, this museum makes an interesting diversion, with lots of aeronautically inclined apparatus awaiting your perusal. And if the exhibits don't amuse you, the exhibitionist goose-stepping of the naval men on duty in the vicinity is sure to do the trick.

◉ SAO ANTONIO ISLET

Map pp8-9; ⏱ Sun afternoons

If you've the taste for truly local flavour on a Sunday afternoon, venture about 5km northeast of Bogmalo, up to the tiny Sao Antonio islet in the middle of the Zuari estuary, which is joined by a thin isthmus to the mainland. Here, at low tide, hundreds of locals converge to pick clams, wading waist-deep into the muddy tidal waters, accompanied by copious quantities of feni (liquor distilled from coconut milk or cashews) and general merrymaking.

DO

✈ BOAT TOURS & WATER SPORTS *Daytrips, Water Sports*

Map p91; jet skis per 15min Rs 900, water-skiing per 10min Rs 800, 1hr 30min dolphin-watching boat trip per person Rs 500

Bogmalo's little beach (see left) is dotted with water-sports vendors offering boat trips, waterskiing and jet skiing out into Bogmalo bay. Outfits change seasonally, so look about for what's on offer, and negotiate hard to get the very best rate.

✈ GOA DIVING *Diving*

Map p91; ☎ 2555117; www.goadiving .com; guided dives from Rs 1430, courses from Rs 15,000

A reputable dive school that offers a host of Professional Association of Driving Instructors (PADI) courses, guided dives and other underwater adventures. This is a great place to begin your love affair with all things beneath the sea.

⚑ EAT

⚑ COCONUT CREEK
Snacks, Drinks $$

Map p91
This swish place, a relaxed set of upscale bungalows set back from the beach, makes for a welcome break from the hassle of the Bogmalo beachfront. Stop in for a quick drink or snack at its terrace cafe (at suitably inflated hotel prices) en route to the airport.

⚑ FULL MOON CAFÉ
Indian, International $$

Map p91
A friendly, basic dining option at the southern end of Bogmalo Beach, which offers good Indian, passable Chinese and fresh sea-food dishes, along with cold soft drinks and beer. Full Moon can also arrange boat trips: ask one of the brothers who run the joint for details.

VELSAO & AROSSIM

◉ SEE

◉ AROSSIM BEACH
Map p91
Quiet and clean, Arossim, like Velsao, is a good place to settle into solitude with a good book.

Here, the simple Starfish Beach Shack is the only place for drink or lunch, and its sunbeds and beach umbrellas occupy a very quiet patch. To get to the beach, follow signs for the Heritage Village Club, and then hop across the sandbags over a rather desultory creek.

◉ OUR LADY OF REMEDIOUS CHAPEL
Map p91
It's the views, rather than the plain little chapel itself, that should entice you to take the steep road east off the coastal road up to Our Lady of Remedious at the top of the hill. On clear days, you'll have a gorgeous, camera-clicking view south along the calm, quiet sands – as long as you studiously ignore the uglier northerly and easterly views up towards the monstrous fertiliser factory and surrounding industrial sprawl.

◉ VELSAO BEACH
Map p91
Despite the gloomy presence of the vast and looming Zuari Agro chemical plant to the north (something in which a Goan Montgomery Burns must surely have had a hand), Velsao Beach makes for a quiet place to get away from it all in the company of just a lifeguard, a scattering of tourists and a flock or two of milling sea birds. The beach road travels through

thick coconut groves past dozens of old bungalows, whilst the coastal road around this stretch makes for a delicious countryside drive, fringed with lily pad–studded lakes and paddy fields, and coconut groves stretching gently down to the sea.

 DO

SERENO SPA
Spa, Alternative Therapies
Map p91; ☎ 2721234; www.goa.park .hyatt.com; Park Hyatt Resort & Spa; facials & massage from Rs 900
Voted 'World's Number One Spa' by *Condé Nast Traveller* magazine readers in 2006, this vast spa, spread over a series of stunning outdoor pavilions, offers a wide

range of ayurvedic and yoga-inspired therapies, treatments and packages. Float away with its Synchronised *Abhyanga* – or 'four-hands' massage – performed simultaneously by two therapists, or ease into the day with a *Khapa Shamak* morning treatment.

 SHOP

THE TREASURE *Antiques*
Map p91; ☎ 2754228; thetreasure@ rediffmail.com; Arossim Beach Rd, near Heritage Village Club, Arossim
If you're a fan of the gorgeous Goan vintage furniture that graces many of the state's old homes and higher-end hotels, pick up your own pieces here from a selection that ranges from dripping chandeliers to carved four-poster beds. Don't miss the small shrine-like chapel on this converted mansion's staircase, a feature that graces the very best of Goa's colonial homes.

 EAT

CASA SARITA *Goan* $$$
Map p91; ☎ 2721234; www.goa.park .hyatt.com; Park Hyatt Resort & Spa; ☽ dinner
Gorgeous upmarket Goan cuisine is dished up at this fantastic hotel restaurant, which offers the piquant flavours of the region's specialities in all their glory. Make

ON THE BALL
Aside from beach volleyball and cricket, which Goans young and old play with equal amounts of regularity and delight, the state sport of choice is football (soccer), and you'll rarely go a day without seeing some local group having a kick on a parched or makeshift football field. Every village has its own team, with players combining to form several national-level teams. Look out for Dempo SC, Churchill Brothers SC and Salgaocar SC, the main players, whose matches are frequently shown on local TV and are best observed in a local bar over a nice cold beer.

or the *vindalho* or the Kingfish curry and you won't be disappointed.

UTORDA

 ## SEE
UTORDA BEACH

Map p91

A clean, if slightly characterless stretch of beach, Utorda makes for a pleasant afternoon. Approach via sandbag stepping stones and rickety bridges over a series of fairly stagnant pools, and take your pick from a ragtag bunch of beach shacks, most of which come equipped with sunbeds. Like Arossim and Velsao further north, the pretty coast is offset by the hulking Zuari Agro chemical plant, but it's nevertheless popular with holidaymakers from the surrounding swish resorts, and comes equipped with a functioning lifeguard.

 ## DO
BOAT TRIPS *Daytrips*

Map p91

Daily fishing and dolphin-watching trips are in no short supply in Utorda; ask around at the beach shacks that line the main stretch of sand and take your pick from the seasonal offerings.

 # EAT
MALLIKA *Indian* $$$

Map p91; The Kenilworth, Utorda;
🕑 **7-11pm**

'Northern frontier' fine-dining courtesy of the swish Kenilworth resort. Mallika's the place to come for succulent kebabs, thick, fluffy tandoori-oven breads and other Punjabi- and Kashmiri-inspired delights.

 ### ZEEBOP BY THE SEA
Seafood $$

Map p91; opposite The Kenilworth;
🕑 **10.30am-11.30pm**

Renowned for its excellent seafood – or 'underwater treasures', as the restaurant describes its cuisine – simple Zeebop, just back from Utorda's main beach, is a firm favourite with locals in the know.

MAJORDA

SEE
MAJORDA BEACH

Map p91

Approached through pleasant, leafy Majorda village, Majorda Beach is a smarter, more organised option than neighbouring Utorda. Here, the stagnant streams and puddles that blight the division between road and beach have been arranged to form a moat which flows round into a pleasant stream, forded by small bamboo bridges. The beach itself comes equipped with half a dozen Russian-dominated beach shacks, all serving up the standard beach menu. To get here, take the left-hand curve of the beach approach; the right-hand curve takes you down to Majorda Beach Resort.

DO

HORSE RIDING
Adventure Sports
Map p91; ☎ 9822586502; 20min ride Rs 200, advanced rider's outing Rs 2000
Keen equestrians shouldn't pass up the opportunity of a sunset or sunrise ride along Goa's rangy sands, and Majorda is currently the only place in the state to do it. Advance bookings with Frank, the proprietor, are essential.

TREAT YOURSELF HEALTH CENTRE
Alternative Therapies, Swimming
Map p91; ☎ 9850183319; gym & pool per day from Rs 100, 1hr massage Rs 700; ⏰ 6am-9pm
This spick-and-span little place in the heart of Majorda village offers a well-equipped gym, swimming pool and ayurvedic-massage centre, run by British expat, Janine. To get here, turn left off the beach approach road.

EAT

GREENLAND BAR & RESTAURANT
International, Goan $$
Map p91; ⏰ 10am-10pm
On Majorda's southern 'Cabana Beach', across a little bamboo bridge, you'll find cute Greenland, run by a sweet British expat couple from Kent. The Goan chef cooks up a range of local specialities including *xacutis* and *vindalhos*, along with yummy banana fritters, however the couple are probably proudest of their spotlessly clean toilet! You'll find Frank's steeds (see left) resting up just outside the restaurant.

RAJ'S PENTAGON RESTAURANT AND GARDEN PUB *International, Indian* $$
Map p91; opposite Majorda Beach Resort; ⏰ noon-midnight
There's decent garden dining at this large, friendly place, worth stopping off at for a filling lunch or evening drink. Located on the right hand side as you head to the beach

BETELBATIM

 ## SEE

BETELBATIM BEACH
Map p91
Betelbatim's sands, just to the north of Colva, are a good

example of what difference a few hundred metres can make, as calm, quiet and pastoral as Colva's (see p98) are touristed and dust-down. Betelbatim itself consists of several different smaller strips of beach – try Lovers' Beach, which is suitably lovely and deserted enough for a spot of romance. To get to Lovers' Beach, follow the signs from the main coastal road, passing a less lovely rash of time-share holiday-apartment buildings on the way.

EAT

MARTIN'S CORNER
Goan, Indian $$

Map p91; www.martinscornergoa.com;
⏱ **11am-3pm & 6.30-11pm**

A local legend and popular with Indian tourists, Martin's Corner is a fine place to try out Goan cuisine. The *xacutis* and *vindalhos* here are superb, and there are plenty of tasty vegetarian options on offer. There's live music most nights from 8pm; plump for, or avoid,

Betelbatim's Martin's Corner is a popular place for live music and a spot of karaoke

Wednesdays, depending on your relationship with karaoke.

COLVA

 SEE

COLVA BEACH
Map p98

If it's a beach paradise you're after, you'll likely be disappointed with what's waiting to greet you in Colva. A large concrete roundabout marks the end of the beach road and the entrance to the beach, and is filled with daytrippers and listless hawkers. The main beach drag is lined with stalls and shabby cafes; sure, it's got all the material needs you're seeking, but as far as atmosphere goes, it's sorely lacking. Still, it makes a decent break if you're pottering along down the coast, or are in need of a water-sports fix (see opposite).

GOA ANIMAL WELFARE TRUST INFORMATION CENTRE & OFFICE
Map p98; www.gawt.org; below Infant Jesus Church Hall; ⏰ **9.30am-1pm & 3-5pm Mon-Sat**

COLVA & BENAULIM

Tate Sports Bar
Sunset Bar
Sagar
Kinara
Water Sports & Dolphin Watching
Colva Beach Rd
Mickey's
Colva Beach
Street Food Stalls
Cafe Coffee Day
Goa Animal Welfare Trust Shop
Our Lady of Mercy Church
Goa Animal Welfare Trust Information Centre & Office
Sal River
Colva
Colva Rd
ARABIAN SEA
Benaulim Village
Blue Corner
Pedro's Bar & Restaurant
Johncy Water Sports & Dolphin Watching
Vasvaddo Beach Rd
Football Ground
Malibu
Holy Trinity Church
Benaulim Beach

0   600 m
0   0.2 miles

THE MENINO JESUS MIRACLE

Inside Colva's 18th-century Our Lady of Mercy Church, closely guarded under lock and key, lives a little statue known as the 'Menino' (Baby) Jesus, which is said to miraculously heal the sick and which only sees the light of day during the Festival of Fama de Menino Jesus, on the second Monday in October. Then, the little image is paraded about town, dipped thoroughly in the river, dressed up for the occasion, and installed in the church's high altar, where miracle-seeking pilgrims arrive in their hundreds to offer prayers and supplications.

t's worth stopping off at Colva if only to drop into this information centre, staffed by volunteers, to find out about the work of this organisation. See p128 for more details.

🏃 DO

🏄 WATER SPORTS & DOLPHIN WATCHING
Water Sports, Daytrips

Map p98; parasailing per ride Rs 500, et skiing per 15min Rs 700, dolphin-watching trips per person around Rs 250
Colva's beach entrance throngs with young men keen to sell you parasailing, jet-skiing and dolphin-watching trips. There's little to choose between operators so you'll have significant leeway in terms of haggling for the best deal.

🛍 SHOP

🛍 GOA ANIMAL WELFARE TRUST SHOP *Charity Shop*

Map p98; www.gawt.org; Colva Beach Rd; ⏰ 10am-12.30pm & 5-7pm Mon-Sat
Another outlet for this charitable concern (opposite); borrow books from its lending library, and peruse the selection of new and second-hand goods on offer.

🍴 EAT

🍴 CAFÉ COFFEE DAY
Snacks, Drinks $$

Map p98; ⏰ 8am-midnight
A pleasant enough place to escape the heat, this wannabe sleek joint offers a half-decent coffee along with a range of sandwiches and cakes, including the suitably '70s Black Forest Gateau, reminiscent of the era when Colva could conceivably have been cool.

🍴 MICKEY'S *International* $$

Map p98; Colva Beach Rd
An ever-popular place to drink the afternoon away or munch on lunch from the extensive Indian, Continental and Chinese menu, Mickey's is usually busy and the food dispensed is fresh and filling.

🍴 SAGAR KINARA *Indian* $

Map p98; Colva Beach Rd
A 'pure-veg' restaurant with tastes to please even committed

BEACHES & TOWNS

COLVA, BENAULIM & AROUND

Colva's Our Lady of Mercy church (p99)

carnivores, this great place is clean, efficient and offers cheap and delicious North and South Indian cuisine all day long.

STREET-FOOD STALLS,
Snacks, Drinks $

Map p98; Colva Beach Rd; ⏱ **from sunset**
Meander along, come sunset, to the eastern reaches of Colva's beach road, and you'll be faced with lots of grilling and sizzling at a string of street-side stalls. Pick up a portion of whatever takes your fancy to fuel your onward wanderings.

DRINK
SUNSET BAR *Hotel Bar*
Map p98; www.soulvacation.in;
Soul Vacation Hotel
A little too trendy for Colva, this white, clean, minimalist place is the Goan outpost of Delhi's famously hip Shalom bar, and is a suitably self-consciously cool place for a cool, cool drink.

TATE SPORTS BAR *Bar*
Map p98; ⏱ **8am-midnight**
You'll find hearty English breakfasts, draught Kingfisher on tap and football on TV at a comfier, more cosmopolitan drinking option than Colva is used to.

BENAULIM
SEE
BENAULIM BEACH
Map p98
A long stretch of largely empty sand, peppered with a few hawkers and stray dogs, laid-back, windswept Benaulim has the distinct feeling of an off-season Welsh seaside resort (were global warming ever to get that far). That said, it's a reasonable enough place to relax on the sands, with a lifeguard present and plenty of sunbed-equipped beach shacks lining the stretch to the north

of the main beach entrance. It
might not be tropical bliss, but it's
definitely decent.

DO

WATER SPORTS & DOLPHIN WATCHING *Water sports*

Map p98; parasailing per ride around Rs 1500; jet-skis per 15min Rs 900, water-skiing per 10min about Rs 800

Like Colva just up the coast,
Benaulim has no shortage of
water sports and boat trip operators, who will likely find you even
before you find them. As always,
negotiate for the best possible
rates.

EAT

BLUE CORNER *Beach Shack* $$

Map p98

The beachfront restaurant comes
heartily recommended by holidaymakers at its adjoining Blue Corner
beach huts, and serves good seafood, Indian and Continental fare
with a great view of the waves.

JOHNCY *Beach Shack* $$

Map p98

Like Pedro's (right) right beside it,
Johncy dispenses standard beach-
shack favourites from its location
just back from the sands themselves. Staff are obliging and food,
if not exciting, is fresh and filling.

MALIBU RESTAURANT
International, Indian $$

Map p98; lunch & dinner

With a secluded garden setting,
this place, a short walk back
from the beach, offers one of
Benaulim's more sophisticated
dining experiences, with great
renditions of Italian favourites,
and live jazz and blues on Tuesday
evenings.

PEDRO'S BAR & RESTAURANT *Beach Shack* $$

Map p98

Set amid a large, shady garden
on the beachfront and popular
with local and international tourists alike, Pedro's offers standard Indian, Chinese and Italian
dishes, as well as a good line in
Goan choices and some super
'sizzlers'.

VARCA, CAVELOSSIM & MOBOR

SEE
CAVELOSSIM BEACH

Map p91

Cavelossim village, a straggling
strip of jewellery and souvenir
shops with a strange proliferation
of dentists, is a place of large,

BEACHES & TOWNS

COLVA, BENAULIM & AROUND

down-at-heel hotels and apartment complexes, strung along the main road. It's here that browsers shop for sandals and sarongs, and the two-week brigade settle in to their plain back-from-the-beach abodes. For all that, though, the beach remains long, wide and beautiful, dotted with water-sports vendors and beach shacks, and a nice place for a paddle.

MOBOR BEACH
Map p91
It's hard to say where Cavelossim ends and Mobor begins, but the further south along the sands you go from Cavelossim proper, the quieter things get. By the time you reach the lush, landscaped Leela hotel, you know you're in Mobor, and the sands quickly head towards the tip of the peninsula where the River Sal meets the sea, and you'll be guaranteed beachside bliss.

OLD ANCHOR HOTEL
Map p91; Cavelossim
Allegedly the first ever resort in south Goa, Cavelossim's decrepit Old Anchor is worth a scooter-ride past on the road down to Mobor, solely for its extreme Las Vegas outskirts–style kitsch value, shaped to resemble a huge boat. Ahoy there, me hearties.

VARCA BEACH
Map p91
Varca, a seemingly endless palm-backed strip of sand (punctuated here and there by the grounds of a luxury resort or a whitewashed Christian shrine), is quiet, calm and almost entirely hawker-free, making it easy to find a quiet spot all to yourself. Outside the resorts, one good access point is the portion known as Zalor Beach; follow signposts from Varca village, near the church. 'You are being watched,' declares a final sign when you arrive, 'No spitting or abusing children.'

DO

BETTY'S PLACE BOAT TRIPS
Daytrips
Map p91; ☎ 2871456, 2871038; Cavelossim; dolphin & birdwatching trip Rs 750, 2hr birdwatching trip Rs 250, multiday scuba excursions Rs 12,000-22,000
A restaurant by night, Betty's offers a wide range of boat cruises by day, including a full-day dolphin and birdwatching trip (price includes lunch and drinks), fishing trips, sunset boat rides and a two-hour birdwatching trip on the River Sal (departing daily at 4pm). It can also arrange multiday scuba excursions to Pigeon Island, in the neighbouring state of Karnataka (price is all inclusive). Drop in or call in advance to book your boat trip.

⛴ FERRY TO ASSOLNA *Ferry*

**Map p91; Cavelossim; pedestrian/
motorbike/car free/Rs 4/7; ⏱ every
10min 8am-8.30pm**

If you're heading down this
coast under your own steam or
just feel in the mood for a nice
boat ride, cross the Sal River at
Cavelossim, by taking the rusting
tin-tub ferry. To reach it, turn east
at the ferry timetable sign, near
Cavelossim's whitewashed church,
then continue on for 2km to the
river. Outside operational hours,
you can charter the ferry to hop
cross to the opposite shore for a
princely Rs 50.

Head across the Sal River to Assolna by ferry

🛍 SHOP

🛍 SAGA *Department Store*

Map p91; ⏱ 9am-9pm daily; Cavelossim
Big-name brands, including Levi's
jeans and bubblegum-bright
Crocs, are available here for half
(or even less) the price you'd pay
in Europe, and the ice-cold air-con
is a distinct draw for browsing
on a hot and sticky summer
afternoon.

🍴 EAT

🍴 BLUE WHALE
Beach Shack $$

Map p91; Mobor
Stray beyond the luxury Leela
(below) to the end of the Mobor pe-
ninsula and you'll be rewarded with
one of the most picture-perfect
spots in the whole of Goa. This is a
simple beach shack with an exten-
sive all-day menu, run by friendly
local Roque Coutinho (p104).

🍴 LEELA KEMPINSKI
Indian, Italian $$$

Map p91; www.theleela.com; Mobor
If you've the taste for luxury,
the opulent Leela is the place to
indulge it. Go for upmarket Indian
and Goan cuisine at its signature
Jamavar restaurant, or alfresco on
the banks of the River Sal at River-
side, which serves delicious Italian
dishes along with a good dollop of
La Dolce Vita.

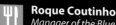

Roque Coutinho
Manager of the Blue Whale beach shack (p103), Mobor

How long have you worked in tourism? My first job was at a beach hut in Benaulim in 1986. I then worked in Palolem for many years, next at the Le[hotel (p103), and finally opened this place a year ago. **Has Goa changed in that time?** Incredibly! I knew Palolem when there were only 'pig toilets where pigs dispense of the contents, and four rooms for rent, for Rs 15 ea[No one there even owned a bicycle – let along a car. **Why did you choos[Mobor?** It's quiet, and we get fresh fish from the migrant fishermen – though I have to be up at 3am when the catch comes in. **Migrant fisher-men?** They're drawn to Goa with tales of wealth but they're very poor, so try to help: we give them a fair price, and little things they need. Toothbru[es, rice, things like that. In India, every little bit counts.

🍴 PAPA JOE'S *Goan* $$

Map p91; Orlim; ⏱ 11am-3pm & 7-11pm

'Nothing fancy, just friendly', say the Papa Joe folks who serve great, spicy Goan cuisine in a friendly open-air restaurant at Orlim, situated just north of Cavelossim on the eastern side of the coastal road. Even the seafood seems happy to be there: its lively specialities include 'laughing squid' and 'jumping prawns'. And if the publicity blurb is to be believed, they've been chefs to the stars: 'Lovely Music Best Food,' allegedly said David Beckam [sic] of UK.

🍴 RICE BOWL *Chinese* $$

Map p91; Cavelossim; ⏱ 10am-3pm & 6-9pm

A simple, small place with an extensive Chinese menu, Rice Bowl offers tasty fuel for a day on the Cavelossim beaches, with great chow mein and vegetable Peking rice.

⭐ PLAY

⭐ JAZZ INN *Music*

Map p91; ☎ 9422437682; Cavelossim; ⏱ 11am-late

With a cosier, more alternative vibe than Cavelossim's standard assortment of tourist bars and beach shacks, this wooden place, tucked off the main drag, serves up live music on Tuesday, Wednesday and Saturday evenings, blending classical, jazz fusion and other styles with great food and strong drinks.

>PALOLEM &
THE SOUTHERN BEACHES

Considered by many visitors to be the most beautiful part of the state, Goa's stretch of southern coast running from Betul down to largely forgotten Polem in the very south, is a beach-lover's dream of golden sands, gentle surf, and the mellowest vibe imaginable. Here you'll find emerald paddy fields studded with egrets and bright-saried farm workers, lazy rivers, herds of wandering oxen, and hidden beaches almost entirely without the big resorts, sprawling hotels or frenzied nightlife of elsewhere.

Palolem, the area's principal beach destination – sporting a simply glorious crescent beach – elicits varied responses from travellers: some lament the hidden bolthole it was in yesteryear, and refer to its modern manifestation as 'Palaga' in reference to a certain popular Mediterranean tourist trap. Others revel in the combination of coco-huts and comfort, enjoying the benefits of a backpackers' paradise where all need not necessarily be shoestring. Either way, the beaches surrounding Palolem, as well as the gentle country lanes connecting them, are as intoxicating as they come.

PALOLEM & THE SOUTHERN BEACHES

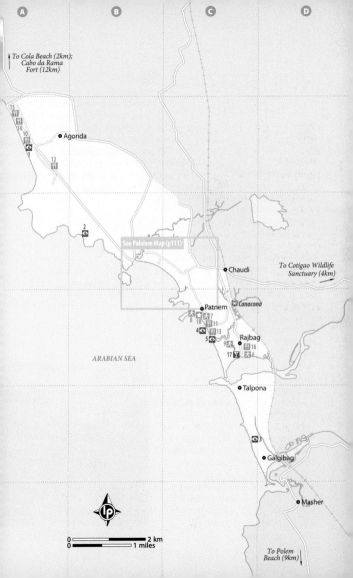

To Cola Beach (2km);
Cabo da Rama
Fort (12km)

15

14
10

● Agonda

12

2

See Palolem Map (p111)

● Chaudi

To Cotigao Wildlife
Sanctuary (4km)

● Patnem   ▣ Canacona

8   7
18   11
4   13
5

Rajbag

9   16
17   6

ARABIAN SEA

● Talpona

3

● Galgibag

● Masher

0   2 km
0   1 miles

To Polem
Beach (9km)

NORTH OF AGONDA

👁 SEE
👁 BETUL

Map pp8-9

A small, sweet workaday village hugging the Sal River estuary, Betul will be your introduction to southern Goa if you're heading down the coast via the Candolim ferry. There are few specific sights here, but it's worth climbing up to the cross-topped Baradi Hillock viewpoint, especially for sunset, to see the glorious southern beach stretching off into the distance.

👁 CABO DA RAMA FORT

Map pp8-9

A fort, named after the god Rama of the Hindu Ramayana epic fame, has occupied this bluff guarding the mouth of the Sal River for centuries, and came into Portuguese possession in 1763. Used as a prison until about half a century ago, there's not much to see these days, though the drive through thick coconut forests is a real treat, and it's without doubt a windswept and melancholy spot with a couple of cold-drinks stalls at the entrance, a luxury the poor Portuguese surely never had.

👁 COLA BEACH

Map pp8-9

Faded signs from the main coastal road direct you down to hidden Cola Beach. Park, and hike down over the headland to get to this quiet, picturesque cove equipped with just one rustic beach-hut operation and a whole lot of blissful solitude.

AGONDA

👁 SEE
👁 AGONDA BEACH

Map p107

Generations of marine turtles can't be wrong – Agonda's beach

Spectacular views from Cabo de Rama Fort

s simply divine; wide, quiet and
picturesque, with a turtle centre
n the middle protecting precious
Olive Ridley (p43) eggs. This is
not, however, the place for a
leisurely swim; the beach shelves
steeply at high tide and the surf
can be rough, but for a sunset
walk or a long lazy day, Agonda
encapsulates romantic Goa at its
very best.

 # DO

 **YOGA, MEDITATION &
AYURVEDA**
Alternative Therapies, Yoga
Agonda's becoming popular, of
late, for its range of foreigner-run
yoga, meditation and ayurveda
options, and you'll find no end
to the daily classes and courses
on offer. Keep an eye out for
signs posted around the Fatima
Restaurant (below), and on lamp
posts and telegraph poles the
length of the beachside road, for
the season's latest set-ups.

EAT

FATIMA RESTAURANT
International, Goan $
Map p107
Terrific lunchtime thalis (complete
meals, served on tin plates) are the
trademark at this teensy local place
with just three tables, a few doors
down from Agonda's whitewashed

church. Its tiny kitchen also dishes
up a delicious *bhaji-pau* (a small,
spicy curry) for breakfast, yummy
fried rice, spaghetti and delicious
finely chopped salads.

LA DOLCE VITA *Italian* $$
Map p107; ⏲ **from 6.30pm**
The best pizzas in south Goa are
to be found at this chequered-
tableclothed place, suitably
popular with an Italian crowd,
along the bumpy road leading
south along the Agonda shore.
Pastas are great here too – and
for something sweet, go for the
'fresh cream cake', a strange, yet
not unpleasant, shade of mint
green.

⊞ SANDY FEET *Beach Shack* $$
Map p107

This mellow beach shack set on the northern portion of Agonda Beach serves up great general beach-shack grub, but its specialities are of the distinctly mountainous variety: tasty *momos* (Tibetan dumplings), Nepali pumpkin curries and an eye-wateringly spicy Nepali peanut salad are the dishes to look out for – if, that is, your eyes stop watering long enough.

⊞ TURTLÈ LOUNGE
Beach Shack $$
Map p107

The impeccably designed Turtle Lounge, just next door to the Sandy Feet, is a flurry of draped fabric, pot plants and carefully placed statuettes. Though there are only two beach huts up for grabs for overnight stayers, its bar-restaurant makes for a highly stylish stop.

PALOLEM

👁 SEE
👁 PALOLEM BEACH
Map p111

Love or hate its recent growth in popularity, it's impossible to deny that Palolem – despite the development that has seen an unbroken string of beach shacks and huts spring forth from one end to the other – remains a beautiful beach. Its southern end tends to be busier, whilst its northern stretch, bounded at high tide by the mouth of a shallow river, is quiet and calm, with a pretty island that you can walk out to at low tide. The sea here is usually shallow and swimmable, and you'll sometimes spot dolphins cavorting in the bay. Beware, however, the weekends, which see scores of local daytrippers descend with their cameras a-clickin'.

🏃 DO

🏃 BHAKTI KUTIR
Alternative Therapies, Yoga
Map p111; www.bhaktikutir.com

Palolem is the place to be if you're keen to yoga, reiki, t'ai chi or tarot the days away. There are courses and classes on offer all over town, with locations and teachers changing seasonally. Bhakti Kutir, set back in the forest at the southern tip of Palolem beach, is a jungle hut that offers daily drop-in yoga classes, as well as longer residential courses, but it's just a single yogic drop in the area's ever-changing alternative therapy ocean. Keep your eyes peeled for posters and flyers advertising new classes.

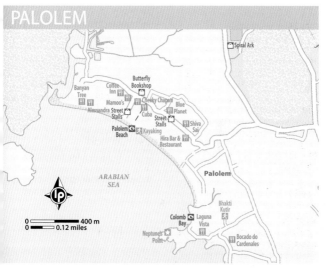

PALOLEM

Spiral Ark

Butterfly
Bookshop

Banyan   Coffee
Tree   Inn
        Mamoo's   Cheeky Chapati
    Alessandra Street   Blue
        Stalls   Planet
                    Cuba   Street
Palolem   Stalls   Shiva
Beach   Kayaking   Sai

        Hira Bar &
        Restaurant

ARABIAN
SEA   Palolem

                            Bhakti
                            Kutir

0 ———————— 400 m   Colomb   Laguna
0 ————— 0.12 miles   Bay   Vista
                                        Bocado do
        Neptune's   Cardenales
        Point

☀ CANOPY ECOTOURS
Daytrips

☎ 9372109987; www.canopygoa.com;
trips per person from Rs 1000

If you're a fan of our feathered
friends, venture out into the wilds
to meet them with Canopy, an en-
vironmentally sensitive operation
also offering unusual butterfly-
spotting, dragonfly-spotting and
wildlife-photography trips. Its
outings will take you to remote
corners of the Western Ghats,
and are highly recommended for
an alternative, and ecologically
minded, introduction to the Goan

countryside. Book your tour either
by phone or online, to arrange
pick-up for your expedition into
the Goan hinterland.

☀ COOKING COURSES
Courses

Look out for local, informal cooking courses, which are slowly
starting to gain ground in the high
season around Palolem. Note that
the options change annually, but
you'll see advertisements for the
current year's culinary choices
posted around and along the main
beach road.

✈ EGYPTIAN DANCE *Courses*
www.katie-holland.net
British expat Katie Holland runs a variety of classes, workshops and intensive courses in and around Palolem, in Egyptian and fusion dance. Check her website or drop her an email for current class details and locations, then get yourself a-shaking and a-shimmying with the best of 'em.

✈ KAYAKING *Water Sports*
Map p111
You'll find kayaks for rent all along Palolem's sands; an hour's paddling will cost around Rs 300, including a life jacket.

✈ T'AI CHI *Courses*
☎ 9923944687
Glen Pelham-Master, husband of belly-dancing Katie Holland (see left), offers a range of courses and classes in the Palolem area, including t'ai chi, personal training, and a host of other techniques; call for details and class locations.

🛍 SHOP

🛍 BUTTERFLY BOOK SHOP *Books*
Map p111; ☎ 9341738801
The best of several good bookshops about town, this cute and cosy place with resident cat stocks best sellers, classics and

Sunset is the perfect time for a stroll along bustling Palolem Beach (p110)

a good range of books on yoga, meditation and spirituality.

SPIRAL ARK
Home Furnishings, Gifts
Map p111
Selling a wide range of fair-trade arts, crafts, textiles and jewellery, along with some unusual organic cosmetic bits and bobs, Spiral Ark, set on the Palolem–Agonda road in an old Portuguese home, makes a great place to pick up a few ethical souvenirs, with an especially good range of children's toys and trinkets.

STREET STALLS *Market Stalls*
Map p111
Street stalls vending faux antiques, clothes, drums and other musical instruments, sandals, sarongs and bikinis all set up in colourful procession all along Palolem's beach-access road, with some great unusual finds in among the usual array if you dig about a bit. Look out for locals selling handmade patchwork blankets in the side streets, festooned from washing lines outside their homes.

EAT
ALESSANDRA *Beach Shack* $$
Map p111
Tucked neatly into the northern end of Palolem Beach, Alessandra churns out probably the best iced coffee in Goa, along with

a lip-smacking vegetarian pad thai, and a pretty decent stab at hummus.

BANYAN TREE
Beach Shack $$
Map p111
One of the best beach bets for Thai specialities, the simple Banyan Tree cooks up tasty Thai curries of the green, red, yellow and potato-and-peanut-rich *massaman* varieties, with regular live music and open-mic sessions several evenings each week.

BLUE PLANET *Vegetarian* $$
Map p111
Tasty vegan and organic treats are served up with love by a local couple at this shady retreat. Bring your water bottles here to be refilled with safe, filtered drinking water for just Rs 3 per litre (free to restaurant patrons), to do your little bit towards reducing Palolem's plastic problem.

CHEEKY CHAPATI
International $$
Map p111
The best time to visit this woodsy, British-run place is after 7pm on a Sunday, when old-fashioned roasts grace the menu, and plates arrive at tables piled high with potatoes, vegetables and all the trimmings. Go for the delicious

SILENCE – I'M DANCING!

In response to Goa-wide ban on loud music after 10pm, Palolem has developed its own distinctive style of partying – that of the quiet kind. Already popular at summer music festivals in Europe, silent parties kit out partygoers with headphones, wirelessly broadcasting music direct to the ear, courtesy of one or two resident DJs. After the call 'To Headphones!' rings out at 10pm, all you subsequently hear from the outside are the shuffles of dancing feet, and the occasional 'Whoo!' when a great song comes on. Locations of parties change annually; check www .silentnoise.in for up-to-date listings.

vegetarian option – a tasty paneer and tofu pie served with red-onion gravy.

🍴 COFFEE INN
International $$

Map p111
If you're craving a cappuccino, roam no further than Coffee Inn, which grinds its own blend of beans to perfection. Its breakfasts are immense, as are its scrummy sandwiches: try the divine smoked-mozzarella kind, which arrives thick with roasted vegetables and pesto.

🍴 CUBA *Beach Shack* $$

Map p111
For scrambled eggs, soups and sundowners alike, perennially popular Cuba, down on the

beach and with a bar on the beach road, has it all. Its Indian food is tasty and filling, as are its Chinese specialities, and the Cuba experience is enhanced by a great music collection, and a laid-back, lazy vibe.

🍴 HIRA BAR & RESTAURANT
Goan

Map p111; 🕒 breakfast
The best place to start the morning in Palolem with a simple *bhaji-pau* and a glass of chai, along with locals on their way out to work.

🍴 MAMOO'S *Indian* $$

Map p111
Don't be put off by the rather dark cavernous interior: Mamoo's is where you'll find Palolem's very best Indian food, in delicious and generous portions. For a taste sensation, explore the variety of vegetarian tandoori options; you'll likely be back the following night to continue trawling the extensive menu.

🍴 SHIVA SAI *Indian*

Map p111; 🕒 breakfast & lunch
A thoroughly local lunch joint, which knocks out tasty thalis of the vegie, fishy and Gujarati kinds. It also does a good line in breakfasts, including banana pancakes (Rs 40).

AROUND PALOLEM

SEE

BUTTERFLY BEACH

ap p107

secluded cove named after its
pidopterous inhabitants. Hire a
ocal boatman at the north end
f Palolem Beach or in Colomb
ay to ferry you up to Butterfly
each and back, relishing the
iews of untouched coastline
long the way. A little further
long, you'll find the even more
ecluded Honeymoon Beach,
lovely narrow strip of sand
unctuated with shade-creating
oulders.

COTIGAO WILDLIFE
ANCTUARY

**ap pp8-9; ☎ 2965601; admission/
mera Rs 5/25; ☼ 7am-5.30pm**

bout 9km south of Palolem,
nd a good option for an early-
orning excursion, is this beauti-
l, remote-feeling sanctuary.
on't expect to bump into its
ore exotic residents (including
aurs, sambars, leopards and spot-
d deer), but frogs, snakes, mon-
eys insects and blazingly plumed
irds are in ample supply. Marked
ails are hikable; set-off early for
e best sighting prospects from
ne of the sanctuary's two forest

watchtowers – though heed the
park warden's recent warning:
'Don't climb too high, madam, for
ladder is under repair.'

COLOMB

SEE

COLOMB BAY

Map p111

Rocky little Colomb might not
be perfect for swimming, but for
examining the inhabitants of low-
tide rock pools, it can't be beat.

Slender palms extend over Colomb Bay

Bring those old-school jelly shoes, though, to avoid shredding your soles on sharp edges.

EAT

BOCADO DO CARDENALES
Spanish $$

Map p111

It's not often you see a Spanish restaurant in Goa, so make the most of a craving for tapas with a trip to this pleasant little restaurant. Especially recommended is the cooling gazpacho, followed by a portion of locally made I Scream ice cream.

LAGUNA VISTA
International $$

Map p111

Great Tibetan *momos* (steamed dumplings) and Nepali thalis can be had at this mellow beach shack, which also offers live music on weekend evenings. Its French co-owner runs informal cooking courses in gourmet French cuisine; ask the staff here for details.

PLAY

NEPTUNE'S POINT *Club*

Map p111

Famous locally these days for hosting Silent Noise parties (see p114), Neptune's Point beach huts, sandwiched between Colomb Bay and Palolem Beach, are also

a hub for various other events, as well as daily yoga classes and courses. Drop in to find out what's on when.

PATNEM

SEE

PATNEM BEACH

Map p107

Smaller and less crowded than Palolem to the north, Patnem makes a quiet and friendly alternative. It's backed by relaxed beach shacks and has a lively surf, making it great for swimming some days and impossible on others, when an equally lively undertow is present. Its main beach road hosts a string of stalls selling the usual variety of clothes, Kashmiri jewellery and trinkets, without the attendant hard-sell of Palolem.

DO

GOA SAILING *Water Sports*

Map p107; ☎ 9850458865; www .goasailing.com

Catamarans are the order of the day at highly professional Goa Sailing, which allows you to build your own itinerary to experience the thrill of sailing these 15ft beauties with or without an instructor. Take an hour's lesson or a daytrip down south, with lunch and impromptu dolphin watching thrown in.

Muskan Komarpanp & Family
Beach hut owners and farmers, Patnem

What's your favourite time of year in Goa? November to April is extremely busy with tourists, so there's no time to rest. My brother sometimes stays up till 4am serving in the bar, and is awake again at 7am to make breakfast. But in the rainy season, everyone finally unwinds. That's the best. **What's the worst thing about the monsoon?** The seas are too rough to fish, so we dry fish in advance. We also dry chillies, collect firewood, dismantle the beach huts, gather hay for the cows and buffalo. Sometimes it rains incessantly for days, so there's lots of hard work to be done before the monsoon actually arrives. **And the best?** It's green, it's calm, it's quiet; everyone has time to spend with each other, with their friends and families. After a nonstop tourist season, there's finally nothing to do but sit back, relax and enjoy.

HARMONIC HEALING CENTRE
Alternative Therapies, Yoga

Map p107; ☎ 2512814; www.harmonicingoa.com

Set high on a hill at the northern end of Patnem Beach and holding regular classes, workshops and treatments – including reiki, yoga, massage, tarot readings and chiropractic treatments – Harmonic is a one-stop centre for all things calming and curative. Consult the website for up-to-date listings on how to get yourself harmonious.

✖ EAT

HOME *International* $$

Map p107

This British-run beach restaurant serves up the best international food in Patnem. Fill up for breakfast with a thick Swiss rosti topped with fried eggs, cheese and tomatoes, or stop in for coffee and a portion of gooey chocolate brownies.

PAPAYA'S *Beach Shack* $$

Map p107

You'll find fine versions of beach-shack food at this friendly Patnem place, which does a great line in masala pappadams (fried pappadams topped with chopped tomatoes, onions, chilli and lime) to accompany a sunset sip. Especially child-friendly, it has often got a paddling pool set up

to keep little ones happy while you're dining.

 # PLAY

MAGIC CINEMA *Cinema*

Map p107

Set up in a coconut grove behind the beach, Magic Cinema screens films on a sizeable open-air screen every evening at 7pm and 9pm, with good Indian food (and perhaps a beer or two) served up alongside

RAJBAG

 # SEE

RAJBAG BEACH

Map p107

Quiet little Rajbag is these days dominated by the presence of the luxury Intercontinental resort, and most of its visitors are consequently hotel guests. It makes for a nice walk, however, from Patnem Beach to the north, clambering across the rocks along the way. Like many beaches in this area, though, beware a treacherous undertow when swimming.

 # DO

FARAWAY CRUISES *Daytrips*

Map p107; ☎ 9850649512, 9828829788; www.farawaycruisesgoa.com

Charter up and cruise the south Goan waters aboard the 18m

WORTH THE TRIP

The workaday inland town of **Ponda** has two big drawcards in the vicinity: Hindu temples and spice plantations, and if either appeal to you, it's well worth a day away from the beach.

The 18th-century hilltop **Manguesh Temple** at Priol, 5km northwest of Ponda, is an architecturally mixed-up composition dedicated to Manguesh, a god known only in Goa, whilst 1km away at Mardol is the **Mahalsa Temple**, also dedicated to a uniquely Goan deity. The 1738 **Shantadurga Temple**, meanwhile, is dedicated to Shantadurga, the goddess of peace, and is one of the most famous shrines in Goa.

One of the best spice plantations to visit is the **Tropical Spice Farm** (☎ 2340329; admission Rs 300; ⏰ 9am-5pm), 5km northeast of Ponda. An entertaining 45-minute tour of the spice plantation, followed by a banana-leaf buffet lunch, is included in the price, and elephant rides (Rs 500) and bathings (Rs 600) are also available.

Nearby, the 200-year-old **Savoi Spice Plantation** (☎ 234 0272; www.savoiplanta tions.com), whose motto is 'Organic Since Origin', is less touristy and elephant-free, but you'll find a warm welcome from knowledgeable guides keen to walk you through the 40-hectare plantation. Local crafts are for sale, and you'll be welcomed with fresh pomegranate juice, cardamom bananas and other organic treats.

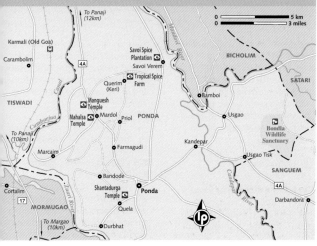

Settle into the cosy atmosphere of Home (p118) on Patnem Beach

wooden boat, *Isla,* which anchors down on the river at Rajbag and takes passengers up to Cabo da Rama Fort (p108) and back, with dolphin watching, lunch and swimming stops along the way. Special itineraries can be arranged for creating that ultimate romantic moment.

🏊 SWIMMING
Swimming Pool
Map p107; Intercontinental Goa Lalit Hotel; 🕑 till dusk
The sleek Intercontinental complex, occupying vast landscaped

grounds, allows nonresidents to use its pleasant outdoor pool for Rs 500 per day. High-priced snacks and drinks are available poolside, and at the swim-up bar.

🍴 EAT
🍴 VERNEKAR RESTAURANT
Indian
Map p107; ☎ 2644649; 🕑 dinner
Ask hanging-out rickshaw drivers the way to this little place down a lane back from the main road past the Intercontinental. It offers a mean tandoori chicken and the world's finest *aloo gobi* (potato and

cauliflower in a spicy masala sauce) for less than the price of a Coke at the hotel itself. Eat along with the locals at one of only four plastic tables: it might be simple, but it serves up some of the very best superspicy grub in south Goa.

DRINK

LOCAL BARS *Local Bar*

Map p107

Venture down to the end of the Rajbag road, which ends abruptly at the banks of the Talpona River, to get your hole-in-the-wall feni (liquor distilled from coconut milk or cashews) fix from one of a range of pokily atmospheric, locally patronised bars.

SOUTH OF RAJBAG

SEE

 GALGIBAG BEACH

Map p107

Gorgeous, deserted Galgibag is one of the last preserves of Goa's endangered Olive Ridley turtles (p43), and is a beautiful pine-backed stretch of deserted sands. Don't come here to swim – undertows and currents are

strong – but it's unsurpassed for a quiet, nature-immersed walk. Stop off for sustenance at the family-run Surya's Beach Café, nestled in the trees, which specialises in seafood, mussels and oysters. Even Gordon Ramsey has allegedly dined – and recommended – this place, as Surya's business card proudly notes.

POLEM BEACH

off Map pp8-9

Goa's southernmost beach, ranged along a beautiful small bay, is seldom-visited but makes a fine spot for a seaside stroll or a picnic on the deserted sands, with a beautiful view of a cluster of rocky islands out towards the horizon. Tourist development hasn't yet made it as far as Polem, and the beach retains a decidedly local feel, with a handful of fishermen bringing in their catch to the northern end and nothing much else to keep you company except scuttling crabs and circling seabirds. For a fishy lunch so fresh it's still dithering, stop at the Kamaxi Hotel among the palms, run by the eccentric local Laxaman Raikar. He also stocks Kingfisher, if you're in need of something cold and frothy.

>SNAPSHOTS

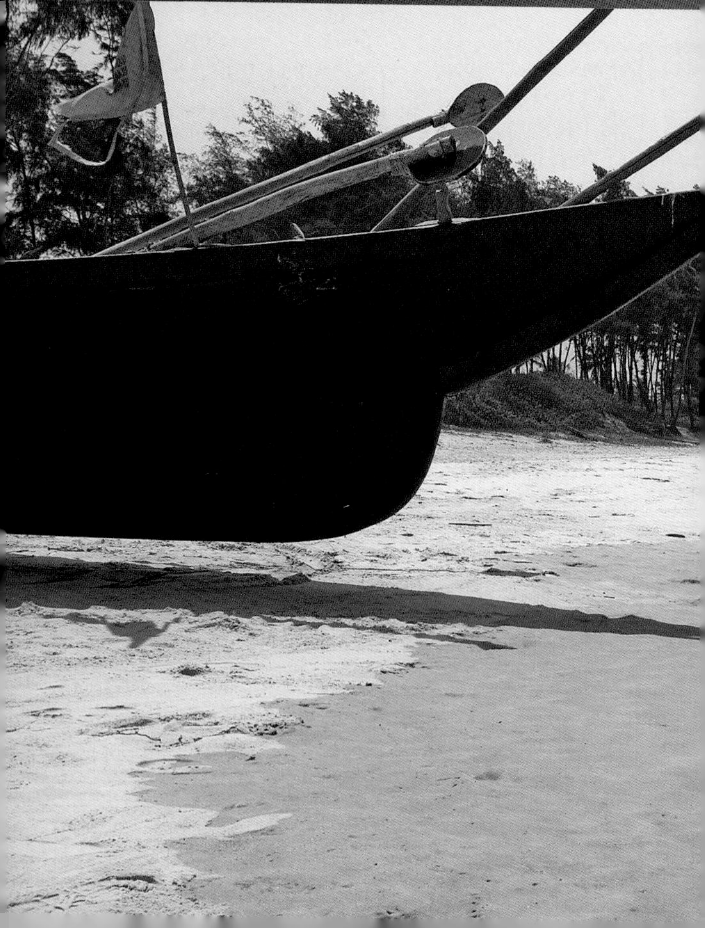

Though it's tempting to spend every postcard-perfect day lazing on the beach, there's far more to Goa than golden sands. Hunt down a festival, explore churches and cathedrals, give a little back or sample glorious local cuisine, to experience every bit of the best the state has in store.

The deserted stretch of Lovers' Beach (p97), Betelbatim

ACCOMMODATION

Whether you're looking for a back-to-basics coco-hut, five-star hospitality, quirky individuality or something somewhere in between, Goa has plenty to cater to all preferences, personalities and pockets.

For those on a shoestring budget, backpacker haunts such as northern Arambol and southern Palolem provide the very best value, with simple huts to be had for just Rs 200 or sometimes even less. The cheapest of this variety consist of little more than bamboo or wooden walls topped with a coconut-palm roof, containing a bed, a mosquito net and perhaps a hammock on a front porch. Many operations change seasonally (with huts removed from the seashore before the arrival of the monsoon rains) so your best, lowest-hassle bet is to take something passable for the first night, deposit your luggage, and then trawl your destination for the hut that suits you best. Generally, the closer to the beachfront, the higher the price tag, though some huts now come equipped with attached bathrooms, hot-water showers, fans, wifi, and other luxuries that are well worth upping your budget to enjoy.

At the other end of the scale, Goa makes a perfect destination for those seeking luxury on their Indian sojourn. The resorts of Candolim and Sinquerim and the southern coastal strip between Velsao and Mobor are dotted with luxurious international-chain operations, many of which offer villa-style accommodation amid landscaped grounds, along with spas, water sports, a bevy of restaurants, and a serene piece of beachfront to top it all off. In Rajbag, the **Intercontinental Goa Lalit** (www.ichotelsgroup.com) is the place for keen golfers, who can tee off right outside their hotel-room door, or for those seeking the fun of the backpacker-heavy Palolem scene with the additional comfort of a feather pillow and turn-down service.

Need a place to stay? Find and book it at lonelyplanet. com. Check out our author reviews and recommendations that cover all budgets from hostels to high-end hotels, as well as more practical information including amenities, maps and photos. Then reserve your room simply and securely via Lonely Planet Hotels & Hostels, our online booking service. It's all at lonelyplanet.com/hotels.

If you're looking for something more charismatic, though, Goa is brimming with personable boutique hotels, many of which are housed in refurbished Portuguese mansions, some in the thick of low-key village life, and others dipping their toes right in the Arabian Sea. Meanwhile, you'll also find a good sprinkling of unusual accommodation on offer: there are tents for rent at **Yoga Magic** (www.yogamagic.net), eco-friendly palm-thatched igloos at **Yab Yum** (www.yabyumresorts.com), whilst the ultimate in Goan escapism can be accomplished at the appropriately named **Elsewhere** (www.aseascape .com).

If dry land doesn't float your boat, consider an overnight stay moored on Goa's backwaters with **Just-A-Saiil's rice barge** (www.justasaiil.com), or on board the Goa Tourism Development Company's similarly characterful three-bedroomed **Santa Lucia** (www.goa-tourism.com). There's much to be said, after a few nights with your feet firmly on warm sand, for messing about on the river.

BEST HERITAGE HOTELS
> Fort Tiracol, Fort Terekhol (www .nilaya.com/tiracol.htm)
> Siolim House, Siolim (www.siolim house.com)
> Vivenda dos Palachos, Majorda (www.vivendagoa.com)
> Hotel Bougainvillea, Anjuna (www.granpasinn.com)

BEST UNUSUAL STAYS
> Yab Yum, Aswem (www.yabyum resorts.com)
> Yoga Magic, Vagator (www.yoga magic.net)
> Elsewhere, Mandrem (www .aseascape.com)
> The Hobbit, Anjuna (www.the hobbitgoa.com)

BEST ROMANTIC RETREATS
> Capella Goa, Parra (www.capellagoa .com)
> Nilaya Hermitage, Arpora (www.nilaya.com)
> Marbella Hotel, Sinquerim (www.marbellagoa.com)
> Casa Susegad, Loutolim (www.casasusegadgoa.com)

BEST LUXURY RESORTS
> Hyatt Regency, Majorda (http://goa .park.hyatt.com)
> Fort Aguada Beach Resort, Sinquerim (www.tajhotels.com)
> Intercontinental Goa Lalit, Rajbag (www.ichotelsgroup.com)
> Leela Kempinski, Mobor (www.theleela.com)

SNAPSHOTS

FOOD

Goan cuisine, with its seemingly infinite combinations of coconut, chillies, rice and spice, is one of the original fusion foods, rich in Portuguese and South Indian heritage. '*Prodham bhookt, magi mookt*', say the locals in their Konkani dialect: 'You can't think until you've eaten well.' With this in mind, tucking in as much and as often as possible should ensure that, by the end of your Goan stay, your head will have cleared like the Arabian Sea in the wake of the monsoon.

Though vegetarian food is in no short supply throughout the state, many Goans, unlike most other Indians, are hearty meat-eaters. With an equally prolific stock of fresh seafood at their disposal, typically Goan dishes come with a meaty or fishy accent. Along with the staple lunchtime fare of fish-curry-rice, a piece of fried mackerel steeped in a thin coconut and red chilli sauce and served with a fluffy mound of rice, another local lunchtime favourite comes in the form of a piled plate of Goan *chouriços*. These air-dried spicy red pork sausages, flavoured with feni (palm liquor), toddy (palm sap) vinegar and chillies, are strung in desiccated garlands from street-side stalls, to be rehydrated, fried up, and served with fresh *pau* bread rolls.

At dinner time, look out for *balchao,* a deliciously rich and tangy dark-red tomato and chilli sauce, often used to cook tiger prawns or fish, and again eaten with fresh bread. Then there's *xacuti*, a spicy sauce – pronounced sha-coo-tee – used originally to create vegetarian dishes ('*sha* means 'vegetable' and *cootee* means 'finely chopped' in Konkani) but also now found in meaty incarnations, which combines coconut milk, freshly ground spices and red chillies.

Chicken and seafood are also frequently basted with *rechead*, a spicy marinating paste which sees its host fried, grilled or baked in a tandoori oven. Dry-fried fish or chicken might otherwise be served spicy *cafrial* style – marinated in a green masala paste and sprinkled with toddy vinegar – or served in a hot-and-sour curry known as *ambot tik*. Meanwhile, the original *vindalho* – far from being the sole preserve of something-to-prove British curry-house lads – is a uniquely Goan derivative of Portuguese pork stew that traditionally combines *vinho* (wine vinegar) with *ahlo* (garlic) and spices.

Sweet stuff, too, is not neglected in Goa. Look out for *bebinca*, a rich and delicious 16-layer coconut cake which is whipped up with sugar, nutmeg, cardamom and egg yolks; *batica*, a squidgy coconut cake best served piping hot from the oven; and *dodol*, a gorgeous, gooey fudgelike treat, made from litres of fresh coconut milk, mixed with rice flour and jaggery (dark sugarcane sugar) and boiled gently for hours on end. They might not be bikini-conducive, but my, don't they taste divine.

For more on Goa's dining scene, see p17.

BEST FOR LOCAL FOOD
> Local cafes, Mapusa Market (p54)
> Street-food stalls, Calangute (p63)
> Sai's Viva Goa!, Candolim (p75)
> Vihar Restaurant, Panaji (p83)
> Martin's Corner, Betelbatim (p97)

BEST FINE DINING
> A Reverie, Calangute (p61)
> Banyan Tree, Sinquerim (p74)
> La Plage, Aswem (p43)
> J&As, Baga (p66)
> Casa Sarita, Arossim (p94)

Top left Colourful spices on show at Anjuna Market (p48) **Above** Street-food vendor, Baga (p63)

GIVING BACK

Though all might seem serene in Goa from your seaside spot, the state has problems like any other. Goa's environment has been heavily burdened by an onslaught of tourism over the last 40 years, but equally by the effects of industry, logging, mining and local customs. Rare turtle eggs have traditionally been considered a delicacy; plastic bottles lie in vast glaciers; and vagrant cows feast on refuse from not-so-fragrant trash cans. Meanwhile, animal shelters overflow with unwanted domestic creatures, and children's homes struggle valiantly to provide shelter, safety

nd education for the state's large population of at-risk and orphaned
hildren.

There are, however, a few easy ways to help. Goa-based children's
harities include **Children Walking Tall** (www.childrenwalkingtall.com) and **El Shaddai**
(☎ 6513286, 6513287; www.childrescue.net), both helping orphans, slum and
treet children. Both accept financial donations to meet specific 'Needs'
sts and offer advice on items you can bring direct from home, even
etailing how to ask your airline for extra luggage space to transport
harity items. Both charities offer child sponsorship, and can arrange
olunteer stints at children's homes in Goa, subject to rigorous vetting
rocedures.

The state's stray animals, meanwhile, are cared for by **International
nimal Rescue** (IAR; ☎ 2268328, 2268272; www.iar.org.uk/india/goa.shtml) and **Goa Animal
elfare Trust** (GAWT; ☎ 2653677; www.gawt.org), the former based in north Goa
nd the latter in the south. Visitors, and financial and practical donations
f things such as newspapers, blankets, puppy toys and flea powder are
elcome at both shelters. Pop in to walk the dogs or play with the pup-
ies, or visit IAR's stall at the weekly Anjuna Flea Market (p48) or GAWT's
hop and information centre in Colva (p98). These are also the people to
ontact if you see an animal in distress whilst in Goa.

Meanwhile, for environmental information, visit the website of the **Goa
oundation** (www.goafoundation.org), the state's main environmental pressure
roup responsible for a number of conservation projects since its begin-
ings in 1986. The increasingly rare Olive Ridley turtles (see p43) that
isit Goa's shores are today protected by the Forestry Department, which
perates huts on Agonda, Morjim and Galgibag Beaches, where turtles
rrive to lay eggs. Drop into these, or go to www.goaforest.com to find
ut more about the department's work.

Other tips for helping out include the following: seek out filtered water
 place of bottled water, or buy bigger, returnable 5L Bisleri mineral-
ater bottles; consider using washable nappies (local laundries are cheap
nd efficient) in place of the disposable kind if you're holidaying with
aby; carry a shopping bag to avoid gathering reams of plastic bags; use
xtra suitcase space on your outbound journey to carry essential items
or donation to charity; save your old newspapers for a dog shelter; and
onsider donating holiday reading and other unwanted items to the
AWT's Colva shop before heading home.

Left Little faces light up alongside a children's shelter volunteer

RELIGIOUS GOA

With Hinduism, Islam and Christianity all represented in Goa, the state offers a rich tapestry of faiths and festivals (p21), with a temple, mosque or church situated seemingly at every turn of its twisting lanes. On Friday mornings, you might hear the melancholy strains of a call to prayer from a lofty muezzin, while on Sundays, the sound of church bells summoning th faithful drifts in across the paddy fields. Hindu festivals regularly illuminate the scene, with the contemplative butter-lamps of Diwali and the riotous colours of Shigmotsav, whilst wayside shrines both Hindu and Christian ar adorned daily by the faithful with candles, flowers and bundles of incense.

What makes Goa unique, however, is the way in which a number of its religious festivals overlap. In December, for example, you'll find Muslims stopping to admire the Christian nativity scenes that spring up beneath the palm trees, and giggling Hindu children in Santa hats stopping to wish you a Merry Christmas.

Though its religious diversity inevitably, from time to time, sparks tensions, Goa's tolerance towards its manifold faiths is an accepted part of daily life, and there's great state-wide dismay whenever a shrine is desecrated or holy relic robbed. In order to experience Goa's religious pantheon, keep your eye out for local celebrations – from a Christian saint's day, through Ramadan, to Hindu *pujas* (offerings or prayers) – anc don't be afraid to glance into a church or temple or two along the way.

BEST TEMPLES
> Manguesh Temple, Ponda (p119)
> Mahalsa Temple, Ponda (p119)
> Shantadurga Temple, Ponda (p119)

BEST CHURCHES
> Church of Nossa Senhora, Mae de Deus, Calangute (p58)
> Church of Our Lady of the Immaculate Conception, Panaji (p78)
> Basilica of Bom Jesus, Old Goa (p88)

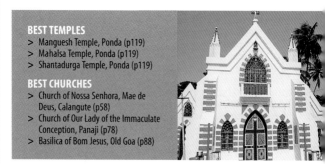

WILDLIFE

All creatures great and small are revealed in their glory in Goa, from the blazing kingfishers that fleck the coastal strip's luminescent paddy fields, to the temple and spice-farm elephants that bestow blessings and elephant rides upon paying visitors.

There's little in life so restful as finding your own deserted stretch of beach and settling in to observe the crabs, gulls, sea eagles and the occasional cavorting dolphin that are so much part of Goa's seaside landscape, or watching the wary tree frog that appears croaking on your balcony each evening.

Goa's wilder expanses, meanwhile, host seldom-seen wonders, such as gaurs (Indian bison), porcupines, wild boar and the occasional pangolin (scaly anteater) or leopard. A loud rustle in the leaves overhead often signals the arrival of a troupe of mischievous langur monkeys, who appear in family groups to steal unattended food from backyards, and generally cause mirth and mayhem.

Taking a riverine trip inland, you might be rewarded with a spotting of wild crocodiles, otters, and yet more birdlife, whose names alone make the trip worthwhile: just try spotting a Ceylon Frogmouth or a Fairy Blue-bird without at least the hint of a satisfied smile.

BEST FOR BIRDLIFE
> Canopy Ecotours (p111)
> Dr Salim Ali Bird Sanctuary (p88)

BEST FOR WILD ANIMALS
> Cotigao Wildlife Sanctuary (p115)
> John's Boat Tours (p71)
> Betty's Place Boat Trips (p102)

V

SNAPSHOTS

GOA WITH CHILDREN

Strolling Goa's sands today, you'll see more visiting children cavorting here than ever before. Goans love children, and your little ones will be greeted with smiles, sweets and treats in abundance – so much so that they might actually grow tired of the constant attention.

Goa's beaches are great for entertaining its younger visitors, with paddling opportunities and rock pools galore, though it's important to heed local advice on the safety of swimming in the sea. Southern Palolem, in particular is a great, safe choice for children, with its gently shelving sands, calm seas, and wadeable river at the northern end.

Beaches, too, are perfect places for satisfying small appetites. Beach-shack menus are long and inclusive, with plenty of familiar Western options for choosy children. Vendors appear at regular intervals dispensing fresh pineapple and coconuts, and there's always a handy ice-cream seller nearby when the need arises.

Though some of Goa's more exclusive boutique hotels don't welcome young guests, you'll largely find hotels and restaurants state-wide well equipped and welcoming for small travellers, and even the simplest of beach huts will be able to rustle up an extra mattress, mosquito net, and hot water by the bucket for showers. Weary parents might also be pleased to know that Arambol, Anjuna and Palolem all have seasonally operating kindergartens, allowing you to grab some quality beach time just like you did back in the good old backpacker days: seek out in-the-know parents when you arrive for details.

BEST BEACHES WITH TODDLERS
> Palolem Beach (p110; pictured right)
> Patnem Beach (p116)
> Baga Beach (p63)
> Arambol Beach (p36)

BEST SAND-FREE PASTIMES:
> Public Observatory, Panaji (p79)
> Spice Farms, Ponda (p119)
> 'Crocodile Dundee' river trip, Candolim (p71)
> INOX cinema, Panaji (p84)

PAMPERING

If you've always longed for that rich-and-famous lifestyle of two massages per day and a facial before breakfast, Goa's the place to achieve it with a price tag a few zeros less than the equivalent in Beverly Hills.

Almost everywhere you go in Goa, you'll be greeted with a plethora of options for ayurvedic massage, which usually involves an hour-long whole-body massage with warm medicated oil, topped off by a steam bath (see p14 for more). You'll also find soothing face treatments, head massages, specialist sports and injury-related massages, and massage courses for couples, where you can test out your newfound skills on your appreciative other half.

If your pampering requirements, however, are of a more hedonistic nature, head to Calangute or Baga to find sumptuous fine dining, wine lists as long as the zinc-clad bar counter, excellent international brand outlets such as Benetton and Wrangler, and even – inconceivably – a shopping mall or two.

But pampering comes in many shapes and sizes in Goa. Check into one of its stellar international hotels (p124) to find your every whim catered to, and every culinary need met. Or go up close and personal with a stay at a boutique hotel, where your hosts may even join you for dinner just to ensure you're pampered in every possible way.

Treat yourself to a luxurious stay in one of Goa's grand colonial mansions

SHOPPING & MARKETS

Goa is blessed with a wide range of shopping opportunities, ranging from the raggle-taggle street-side stalls that tumble along almost every beach approach, through an increasing scattering of high-end 'lifestyle' boutiques, and on to the international brands (think Crocs and Lee Cooper) that line the Calangute–Candolim road and cluster around Panaji's 18th June Rd.

Uniquely Goan souvenirs worth looking out for are *azulejos,* painted Portuguese-style tiles that you'll find lurking in various antique and reproduction shops, and tasty Goan cashew nuts, which you'll find in various grades and prices in any Goan market. Almost every area of India, however, is represented in souvenir shops and stalls: the best carpets come from Kashmir, and the colourfully adorned Lamani tribal women of neighbouring Karnataka state sell cheap jewellery and bright mirrored textiles. Silver jewellery and bright woollens (just perfect for the beach) are the preserve of India's Tibetan minority.

If it's markets you're after, you're in for a treat: head to Anjuna for its Wednesday flea market, and to Mapusa on Fridays for a slice of local, rambunctious market action. And in all circumstances, haggle hard: it's an accepted, even expected, part of the market fun.

BEST HIGH-END BUYS
> Casa Goa, Calangute (p60)
> Fusion Access, Panaji (p81)
> Treasure, Arossim (p94)
> Karma Collection, Baga (p65)

BEST STREET-STALL SHOPPING
> Anjuna Flea Market (p48)
> Mapusa Market (p54)
> Palolem Beach Road (p110)
> 'Glastonbury Street', Arambol (p37)

BARS & DRINKING

Unlike other parts of India, where alcohol may be so taboo that it's served up incognito in a tea pot, there are few restrictions on tipple in Goa. The local drinks of choice include beer (Kings and Kingfisher are both popular and palatable), brandy (Honey Bee being the local cheapie), locally produced wines and rocket-fuel feni.

Feni, its name stemming from the Konkani 'fen' meaning 'to froth,' is a clear liquor distilled from the sap of either coconut palms or cashew trees. To make the fiery former, men known as 'toddi tappers' clamber three times daily up coconut trees, to tap 'toddi', (coconut-tree sap). The toddi then ferments in the sun, and is distilled twice before drinking. Costlier cashew feni, meanwhile, is extracted from the fruit of the cashew tree, before being similarly distilled to create an end product that some hardened drinkers liken to tequila. Both types can be drunk neat, or mixed with water, soda or lemonade-style Limca to soften the blow. For the most atmospheric local experience, pick one of Goa's infinite hole-in-the-wall bars, and try the 'I'll have what he's having' approach.

Pop into a hole-in-the-wall bar in the Sao Tomé quarter (p78) of Panaji

SNAPSHOTS

PARTYING

Goans love to party, at weddings, religious celebrations, and especially during the state's raucous three-day Carnival, which first appeared on the Goan calendar in the 18th century, courtesy of its Portuguese colonisers. Intended to encourage revellers to expend pent-up energies before the sober coming of Lent, Carnival soon became imbued with an unequivocally Goan flavour, and traditional satirical folk plays, known in Konkani as *khells,* have now been performed during Carnival for centuries. Carnival madness kicks off on Sabato Gordo ('Fat Saturday') when a character known as King Momo arrives to decree happiness on all his subjects. The results are inevitably drunken, musical and frenzied.

In contrast to the ebullience of local Goan parties, in recent years staunch noise-pollution laws have signalled the death knell for the once burgeoning and drug-laden international trance-party scene. International partying still goes on here and there throughout the state, though without the frequency of years past: head to Vagator (p52), Chapora (p51) or Anjuna (p46) to wait for word of increasingly rare jungle-trance parties, live it up Ibiza-style at Tito's (p67) in Baga, sniff out what's up at Vagator's Hilltop (p55) or experience the remnants of trance at Vagator's Nine Bar (p55), now open only until a tame 10pm.

The grand exception to the rule, however, can be found in Palolem, where 'silent parties', cunningly employing wireless headphones to circumvent noise-pollution laws, still continue on till the dawn. Check ou www.silentnoise.in for dates and locations.

Tito's (p67) in Baga, a stalwart of Goa's clubbing scene

>BACKGROUND

The Portuguese legacy lives on in Goa's crumbling colonial mansions

BACKGROUND

HISTORY

Though Goa's history of human habitation dates back tens of thousands of years, probably the most influential event in Goan history – the effects of which are still clearly evident today – occurred with the coming of the Portuguese in a relatively recent 1510, who arrived seeking control of the region's lucrative spice routes by way of Goa's wide natural harbours and plentiful waterways. Defeating the ruling Bijapur kings, the Portuguese steadily pushed their power from their grand capital at Old Goa, out into the surrounding provinces.

Soon the conquerors were seeing to it that not only Portuguese rule, but their religion too, was spread throughout the state – by force, if need be – and the Goan Inquisition saw unprecedented repression and brutality in the name of Christianity. Though the Marathas – the central Indian people who controlled much of India at various points in history – almost vanquished the Portuguese in the late 18th century, and despite a brief occupation by the British during the Napoleonic Wars in Europe, it wasn't until 1961, when the Indian army marched into Goa, that almost five centuries of Portuguese occupation finally came to an end in India.

Today the legacy of the Portuguese can still be found almost everywhere, in the state's scores of crumbling mansions, its cuisine, its churches and even in its language; though it's slowly becoming rarer, if you keep an ear out you'll likely hear old people sitting together and conversing in Portuguese during some point in your stay.

AN ARROW MARKS THE SPOT

Hindu legend has it that Goa and its glorious coastline were created by a god named Parasurama, the sixth of 22 incarnations of the god Vishnu, the preserver. The story goes that after many years caught up in avenging his father's murder, Parasurama came to rest on the Western Ghats, the mountain range that forms the natural border between Goa and neighbouring Karnataka state. Seeking a pure place to conduct his fire sacrifices, Parasurama shot his arrow towards the Arabian Sea, commanding it to withdraw to wherever the arrow came to rest. It landed where Benaulim stands today, the sea retreated, and the coastal plain was revealed, ready and waiting for Parasurama.

SUSEGAD

You'll see the word *susegad* (also spelled '*sosegado*') all over the place in Goa; in hotel and cafe names, painted onto the back of trundling buses and, in particular, gracing the lintel of many a grimy local bar.

Susegad, in essence, means taking it easy: not worrying if the thing that was to be done yesterday isn't done until tomorrow, or waiting it out with patience if the road ahead is blocked by a lumbering herd of stubborn water buffalo. Stemming from the Portuguese *sosegado*, meaning 'quiet', it's become a way of life in Goa, and is responsible for the state's long siestas and languid, leisurely charms. Experience a dose of *susegad* for just a day or two, and you'll inevitably want to keep coming back for more.

GOAN LIFE

International tourists aren't the only non-Goans who arrive at the sunny state in search of the good life. The state enjoys one of India's highest per-capita incomes and comparatively high health and literacy rates, factors which attract a good scattering of folks from other parts of India who arrive either to find work, or to seek that magical *susegad* (also known as *sosegado*; see below) they've heard so much about. Some are refugees of the Mumbai rat-race who've given up respectable jobs in law, technology or the business world to pursue their dream of a little restaurant by the sea or a colonial mansion in the hinterland. Others are Kashmiris, Tibetans, Nepalis, Lamanis from Karnataka or migrant workers from Gujarat and Orissa, who come here seeking work in the tourist trade, or labour as fisherfolk and seasonal farm workers in Goa's verdant paddy fields. Sadly, a large proportion of Goa's homeless population are migrants, driven from their homes often due to water shortages, and hoping life here will treat them more kindly. Almost inevitably, it doesn't.

Meanwhile, local life, with its emphasis on religion and family life, generally continues on uninterrupted as it has for centuries. Most Goans, accustomed to long-staying colonisers of one sort or another, take little stock in the rise and fall of visitors: once it was the Portuguese, next came the British and the hippies, and now it's the turn of the package tourists. A shrug of the shoulders and a quick change of the menu – from baked beans to borscht – and it's business as usual for the many Goans who make their seasonal living catering to tourists intoxicated by Goa's charms.

In some historic decaying mansions, though, you'll find relics of another, wealthier Goan class: the ageing remnants of Goa's landed gentry, their ancestors bestowed with land and titles by their Portuguese overlords. Nowadays the descendents struggle with the upkeep of vast and unruly mansion homes and rile against termites, white ants and the inevitable effects of the annual monsoon. 'Things were once better,' lamented one homeowner recently over a steaming porcelain cup of weak Earl Grey. 'We all drove Mercedes, and Scotch Whisky was just Rs 10 a bottle. We drank French wines – white with fish, red with meat – and bought proper cheese, from Holland, France and Italy. Now it's just the monkeys for company, and we haven't used the ballroom for many, many years.'

Back in the simple villages behind the beach, extended families live in close proximity; children are largely considered a familial – rather than purely maternal – responsibility, and village life, with its attendant gossip, is as tightly knit as ever. Children attend village schools with punctuality and keenly starched uniforms, and the whole family has its role in household upkeep. Women in Goa enjoy a higher legal, educational and social status than anywhere else in India, and you'll find plenty of female doctors, vets, lawyers and teachers throughout the state, not to mention some formidable female managers of the state's best-kept beach huts.

MUSIC & DANCE

Listen carefully beyond the lounge, Bob Marley and techno jumble of the beach shacks, and you'll hear Goa's own melodies, which, like most other things in the state, are a heady concoction of East and West.

Goan-style folk music means a song for every occasion: for weddings, funerals, fishing trips and toddi tapping, but music is especially prevalent at festival time, when local agricultural labourers, known as the *Kunbi* class, belt out *Kunbi geet,* songs with the slow, steady rhythms of manual work in the fields. The most famous kind of Goan folk song, however, is the *Mando,* also known as 'the love song of Goa', a slow melody with accompanying dance, which sees its largely Catholic participants dance in parallel lines while flourishing paper fans and handkerchiefs; you might catch a glimpse of this if you pass a Christian wedding or feast day in progress. As the *Mandos* continue, the pace picks up to become peppy dances known as *Dulpods* and *Dekhnis,* their songs filled with biting lyrics that relate the latest gossip from village life, intermingled with renditions of traditional folk tales.

Though increasingly rare in Goa as those of the older generation carry it to their graves, the melancholy, haunting fado can still be heard here and there in Goa. The songs of fado lament lost love, or a longing for a Portuguese home that most singers here, in fact, have never seen. Listen out for the late, great folk singer Lucio de Miranda, or Oslando, another local folk and fado favourite.

Local Konkani pop is a strange and sometimes even wonderful combination of tinny, trilly musical influences: African rhythms and Portuguese tunes, with a bit of calypso thrown in. You'll catch its twangy melodies from passing cars, buses, taxis and in local Goan restaurants and lunch spots. A classic, old-school performer to look out for – who has influenced a whole new generation of local musicians – is Lorna, 'the Goan nightingale', much-loved locally and well worth looking up for her classic Konkani tunes.

The Western music scene in Goa, meanwhile, still thumps – albeit less incessantly than in recent years – to the hypnotic rhythms of Goa Trance, or Psy-trance, which came to prevalence in the early 1990s. Its most famous exponent remains Goa Gil, who DJs trance parties worldwide; go to www.goagil.com to see where he's next appearing – though these days it's unlikely to be in Goa itself.

Aside from local celebrations (to which tourists are often extended a warm welcome), the best places to find traditional music and dance performances are at Panaji's Kala Academy (p84) and Calangute's Kerkar Art Complex (p58). Scan local newspapers, too, for forthcoming concerts. Goa Trance parties nowadays are increasingly few and far between, but drop into Vagator's Nine Bar (p55), Chapora (p51) or Anjuna (p46), and listen out for word of parties.

LISTEN TO THE BAND

Whatever your musical inclinations, it's worth hopping online to get a taste of Goan music in one, or many, of its forms.

> Goa Trance (www.goatranceradio.com) – Head to the Goa Trance radio portal to get your fill of psy-trance.

> Goan Fusion (www.remomusic.com) – Goan export Remo Fernandes is adored throughout India for his heady cultural infusions. Listen to clips, and download a song or two, at his official site.

> Fado and Mando (www.luciomiranda.in) – Revel in the melancholy strains of the late Lucio de Miranda at his official website.

> Konkani Radio (www.live365.com/stations/61664) – Traditional Goan sounds of all kinds can be picked up 24/7 at this internet radio portal.

GOAN ARCHITECTURE

Wherever you are in coastal Goa, you'll never be far from an interesting bit of architecture, whether in temple, church or mansion form. Much of Goa's atmospheric, crumbling, historic architecture is the product of its colonial heritage, and there's no end to the slowly crumbling bungalow mansions, with their wide verandahs, wrought-iron balconies, shady front *balcaos* (pillared porches), oyster-shell windows, and central *saquáos* (inner courtyards), around which family life traditionally revolved.

Most of these grand old buildings were built in the early 18th century, when wealthy Goan merchants and officials were rewarded for their service to the empirical masters with the spoils of a lucrative sea-trade. The architecture, inevitably, was inspired by dominant European tastes, though the materials – red laterite stone, terracotta, oyster shells and wood – were all sourced locally. The houses' contents were often imported, with little luxuries like silk, lace, teak and porcelain brought from far-off exotic climes, including Japan, Macau, Belgium, Venice, and Portugal itself. The most sumptuous of these homes also contained locally crafted wooden chapels, or oratories, which housed gilded and golden relics, and altars and images of Catholic saints as the focal point for family prayers. Today, a walk around the back lanes of Candolim (p68), Siolim (p51) or the coastal stretch from Velsao to Mobor (p90) will yield a treasure-trove of colonial mansions, in various stages of decay or, occasionally having undergone refurbishment. Meanwhile, a visit to Calizz (p70) is another wonderful way to bring yourself up to speed with Goa's architectural heritage.

Churches, too, are the product of Portuguese influence, many of cruciform design and constructed from local laterite stone, whitewashed and plain since laterite is too coarse to support fine carving. In contrast, even the humblest of village churches usually sports a sumptuous interior, with an elaborate gilt *reredos* (ornamented altar backdrop) and lots of carving, painting, chandelier-lighting and other embellishment adorning the altar before it and chancel in front of that. Peek into any village church you come across to be dazzled by light, gilt and colour, and don't miss a stop off at Panaji's Church of Our Lady of the Immaculate Conception (p78), or at Old Goa (p88) for even statelier examples of Goa's Catholic architectural heritage.

Goan temples are yet another form of architectural hybrid, enfolding both Muslim and Christian elements into traditional Hindu designs. Their most unusual and distinctive feature is the unique-to-Goa 'light towers', known as *deepastambhas,* which look a little like Chinese pagodas, and are atmospherically decorated with oil lamps during festival periods. You'll also be able to spot Hindu households during your travels, from the multicoloured *vrindavan* (ornamental container) that stands outside the front of the house. Growing inside it is the sacred tulsi plant. In Hindu mythology the tulsi is identified as one of the god Vishnu's lovers, who his consort, Lashmet, turned into a shrub in a fit of jealousy.

FURTHER READING

English translations of the work of Goan authors are surprisingly scant, though there are a few titles worth seeking out at one of the state's many English-language bookshops. Victor Rangel Ribeiro's *Tivolem,* a series of interlinked Goan vignettes, and *Angela's Goan Identity,* by Carmo D'Souza, are two titles worthy of a beachside read. Meanwhile, *Sorrowing Lies My Land* by Lambert Mascarenhas, first published in 1955, is an engrossing account of Goa's struggle for independence, which began in the mid-1940s.

For historical perspectives on Goa, Victorian adventurer Richard Burton's *Goa and the Blue Mountains* and Gita Mehta's glance at the psychedelic Goan '70s in *Karma Cola,* make a great, contrasting pair, whilst *Reflected in the Water: Writings on Goa* (ed Jerry Pinto) brings together five centuries of writings on Goa, encompassing such literary luminaries as Graham Greene and William Dalrymple.

A host of worthy coffee-table tomes, rich with evocative illustrations, make great buys to warm up those dark winter days back home. *Inside Goa,* by Manohar Malgonkar, with drawings by famous Goan cartoonist Mario Miranda, delves into Goan history, ancestry and identity, while *Best of Goa,* published by Global Village Partnerships, examines its houses, beaches, feasts and heritage in photographic form. For all architecture enthusiasts, the lavishly illustrated *Houses of Goa,* with a foreword by renowned Goan architect Gerard de Cunha and which peeks behind many closed mansion doors, is an absolute must, whilst for background and context, Maurice Hall's well researched *Window on Goa: A History and Guide,* can't be beaten.

In terms of a decent daily read, Goa is home to a prolific and thriving local English-language press. Three newspapers – the *Herald,* the *Navhind Times,* and the local edition of the *Times of India* – are printed here daily. National issues of constant interest include hauliers' strikes, political scandals, the prime minister's health and hyped accounts of tense

THE LIGHTER SIDE OF LITERATURE

Outside the newspapers, look out for the constant supply of misspellings that light up the dullest of standard beach-shack menus – then order a 'bugger' instead of a burger, or 'humans' in place of hummus, as you see fit.

Meanwhile, while out on the roads, don't miss the wealth of pithy roadside warnings, covering everything from forest fires to road safety and entreaties to 'Commit No Nuisance'. A few of our roadside favourites include the following:

> Hurry Hurry, Spoils the Curry
> Drive Fine, Avoid Fine
> Caution and Care Makes Accidents Rare
> Lane Driving is Sane Driving
> Drive with Care – Life Has No Spare
> Driving Rash Causes Crash

'Indo–Pak' relations. Don't count on them, though, to bring you up to speed on international issues, which are generally glossed over with only the most bizarre, gossip-driven or sensational selection of international stories making the cut.

However the most endearing feature of Goan papers – especially the *Herald* and the *Navhind Times* – is the way in which even the most serious or distressing of subjects can be told so engagingly: if only Western broadsheets still regularly used words like 'miscreant', 'gobbledygook', 'tomfoolery', and 'codswallop' when reporting on alleged governmental bribery. Juicier local-news items can keep the holiday reader entertained for hours. Read how locals shockingly tied the public-roads inspector to a large tree in protest of shoddy road-fixing work, or how a body of uncertain gender was eventually discovered inside a foul-smelling barrel at a local railway station's left-luggage department after the barrel was left unopened for 12 months, as per station regulations.

DIRECTORY
TRANSPORT
ARRIVAL & DEPARTURE
AIR

Goa's sole and diminutive Dabolim airport (Map p91, A1) is situated right in the centre of the state, an easy taxi ride (usually two hours, at most) from any of Goa's beaches. Few international flights arrive here, and those that do are package-holiday charters, almost exclusively from Russia and Britain.

Numerous domestic airlines fly in and out of Goa daily, with most flights taking off and landing throughout the morning and early afternoon. Of them, **Indigo** (☎ 1800 180 3838; www.goindigo.in), **GoAir** (☎ 1800 222 111; www.goair.in) and **Spicejet** (☎ 1800 180 3333; www.spicejet.com) are the cheapest, and **Kingfisher** (☎ 1800 180 0101; www.flykingfisher.com) and **Jet Airways** (☎ 1800 225 522; www.jetairways.com) by far the most comfortable.

It's usually cheapest and easiest to book online as far in advance as possible, and any inquiries are best made to the airlines' toll-free numbers in India. Dabolim Airport's arrivals hall is equipped with an ATM, money exchange and tourist-information office. There are two prepaid taxi booths (one in the arrivals hall and the other just outside), at which you pay upfront for taxi rides at fixed, fair prices to any Goan destination.

TRAIN
The **Konkan Railway** (www.konkanrailway.com), the main train line running through Goa, connects Goa with Mumbai to the north, and with Mangalore to the south. Its main train station in Goa is Madgaon station (Map p91, C3) in Margao, from which there are several useful daily services to Mumbai.

CLIMATE CHANGE & TRAVEL

Travel – especially air travel – is a significant contributor to global climate change. At Lonely Planet, we believe that all who travel have a responsibility to limit their personal impact. As a result, we have teamed with Rough Guides and other concerned industry partners to support Climate Care, which allows people to offset the greenhouse gases they are responsible for with contributions to energy-saving projects and other climate-friendly initiatives in the developing world. Lonely Planet offsets all staff and author travel.

For more information, turn to the responsible travel pages on www.lonelyplanet.com. For details on offsetting your carbon emissions and a carbon calculator, go to www.climatecare.org.

Convenient services include the overnight *Konkan Kanya Express (KKE),* which departs Mumbai's Dadar station at 11.05pm, arriving at Madgaon the next morning at 10.45am. In the opposite direction, the *KKE* departs Madgaon at 6pm daily, and arrives at Mumbai's Dadar station at 5.20am. The fastest train from Mumbai is the *Jan Shatabdi Express,* which departs Mumbai's CST at 5.10am and arrives in Madgaon at 2.10pm. In the opposite direction, the *Jan Shatabdi Express* departs Madgaon at 2.30pm and arrives at Mumbai's CST at 11.20pm.

There are plenty of other rail options, too, to other parts of India. The daily *Goa Express* (train number 2780; 16½ hours) and the daily *Rajdhani Express* (train number 2432; 25 hours) both link Madgaon to Delhi's Nizamuddin station. Train bookings are best made at the train-reservation office at Panaji's Kadamba Bus Stand (Map p77, F3) or at any travel agent that sells train tickets (though you'll probably pay a small commission for the convenience). Make sure you book as far in advance as possible for sleepers, as they fill up quickly.

You can also book *Konkan Kanya Express* tickets on the Konkan Railway website (see p145), subject to a long list of conditions: you can only book between seven and two days in advance of travel, only in 3-tier sleeper air-con class for a cost of Rs 1500 per ticket, and with no date changes permitted.

VISAS
Almost every visitor needs to obtain a visa before entering India. This should be done well in advance of travel; check the website of your local Indian consulate or embassy for up-to-date details.

GETTING AROUND
To truly explore the Goan coastal byways, many visitors opt for renting a scooter, or a heavier, revvier Royal Enfield Bullet motorbike. Local buses, though cheap and frequent, often involve being packed in sardine style, and then chugging along at a pace not much faster than a brisk jog. Trains make for a time-consuming means of getting about, and are best employed only if you're arriving in Goa from elsewhere in India.

If you're not keen to travel under your own steam, yellow-and-black autorickshaws will whiz you about locally (Rs 50 for short rides, Rs 100 for longer ones), or you could take your chances on Goan roads on board a bicycle: bikes can be bought or rented nearby every beach, and make the ultimate clean, green method of seeing the countryside.

MOTORCYCLE

You'll rarely go far on a Goan road without seeing an intrepid tourist whizzing by on a scooter or motorbike, and renting (if not driving) one is a breeze. You'll likely pay around Rs 150 to Rs 300 per day for a scooter, Rs 400 for a smaller Yamaha motorbike, and about Rs 500 for a Royal Enfield Bullet.

If you've never biked or scooted before, bear in mind that Goan roads are treacherous, filled with human, bovine, canine, feline, mechanical and avian obstacles, as well as a good sprinkling of potholes and hairpin bends. Take it slowly, try not to drive at night, don't attempt a north–south daytrip on a 50CC scooter, and the most cautious of riders might even consider donning a helmet or shoes.

TAXI

Taxis are widely available for hopping from town to town, and a full day's sightseeing, depending on the distance, is likely to be around Rs 1500 to Rs 2000; you'll rarely find a taxi with a functioning meter. Motorcycle taxis are also a licensed form of taxi in Goa. They are cheap, easy to find, and can be identified by a yellow front mudguard – and even the heftiest of backpacks seem to be no obstacle.

BUS

Goa boasts an extensive network of buses, shuttling passengers to and from almost every tiny town and village. There are no timetables, no bus numbers or fixed fares (though it would be hard to spend more than Rs 20 on any one single journey), and often no official bus stops (just stick out your hand and hope they slow down). In cities like Panaji and Mapusa, head to the Kadamba Bus Stand (Map p77, F3; named after the state's biggest bus company) and scan the signs posted on the bus windscreen to find the service you're after; otherwise ask a driver who'll point you to the right old banger. Anywhere else, wait wherever you see locals doing the same, and ask around for buses to your chosen destination.

CAR

It's relatively easy, if you've the nerves and the skills, to procure a self-drive car in Goa, giving you the (white-knuckle) freedom to explore the region's highways and byways at your own pace. A small Chevrolet or Maruti will cost you around Rs 600 to Rs 900 per day and a jeep around Rs 1000, excluding petrol. Note that there are few organised car-rental outlets, so ask around for a man with a car who is willing to rent it to you.

PRACTICALITIES

BUSINESS HOURS

There are few standard business hours in Goa, except for the rule that most shops and offices shut up shop for siesta for an hour or two daily, sometime between noon and 4pm. Outside siesta, shopping hours can range from 7am to midnight, seven days per week in peak tourist season, shrinking to several hours per day, with Sundays off, at other times of the year.

Generally, banks are open at least from 10am to 2pm, Monday to Friday, and 10am to noon on Saturdays, though ATMs are nowadays almost all 24-hour.

DANGERS & ANNOYANCES

One of the greatest – and most deceptive – dangers in Goa is to be found just beyond your beautiful bit of beach. The Arabian Sea, with its strong currents and dangerous undertows, claims dozens of lives per year, many of them foreign. Lonely Planet has received one letter from a reader whose adult daughter and her friend both drowned whilst paddling in the sea in north Goa.

Though some of Goa's beaches are now overseen by lifeguards during daylight hours, it's most important to heed local warnings on the safety of swimming, and don't, whatever you do, venture into the water after drinking or taking drugs.

Be sure to keep your valuables under lock and key – especially if you're renting an easy-to-penetrate coco-hut – and don't walk along empty stretches of beach alone at night; this is especially good advice for women. Away from the beaches, it makes sense for visitors of both sexes to adopt more modest forms of dress, in-keeping with local customs: avoid bikinis and bare midriffs, and women might feel more comfortable covering their shoulders. At weekends, some Goan beaches see an influx of single Indian men, keen on doing a spot of close-up bikini-watching. It's best to ignore them and refuse to comply with requests to have your photo taken; referring firmly to any of the most persistent individuals as 'My brother' is sure to dampen down a large degree of lustiness. If all else fails, start shouting, and they'll rapidly disperse.

Recreational drugs including acid, ecstasy, cocaine, charas (cannabis or hashish) and marijuana are illegal in India (though still very much available in Goa) and purchasing or carrying drugs is fraught with danger. Goa's Fort Aguada jail is filled with prisoners, including some foreigners, serv-

NO STREET NAMES?

Outside the larger Goan towns of Panaji and Mapusa, it's very uncommon to come across streets blessed with official names. This doesn't, however, make it too difficult to get about, since most coastal villages comprise just a handful of beachside lanes: if in doubt, ask a local or consult our maps.

ing lengthy sentences for drug offences, and being caught in possession of even a small quantity of an illegal substance can mean a 10-year stay in a cockroach-infested cell.

ELECTRICITY

Power cuts are common in Goa, and you might find that unless you're in swish digs with back-up generators, you'll be electricity-free for an hour or so each day. Most electricity is 230V to 240V AC, although this can vary. British, Irish, New Zealand and Australian appliances will need a universal adaptor (bring one from home), and American and Canadian plugs will also need a transformer, unless your appliance is multivoltage.

EMERGENCIES

In any emergency in Goa, dial ☎ 108. This will connect you to the police, fire brigade or medical services.

HEALTH

The majority of travellers to Goa experience few illnesses except for food- or hygiene-related stomach complaints, but it's worthwhile making a quick trip to your local doctor well in advance of travel to check up on advised vaccinations. Though malaria isn't widespread in Goa, do bring along plenty of mosquito repellent for liberal application around sunset, as Goan mosquitoes can be voracious.

Lots of tourist-oriented restaurants nowadays make a point of washing fruit and salad, and making ice from filtered water, but if you have any doubts, steer clear of these things.

Even the smallest Goan villages are equipped with at least a couple of good family doctors: ask at your hotel for details of a general practitioner if the need arises. Meanwhile, an astounding array of medicines can be purchased over the counter in Goa without the need for a prescription.

HOLIDAYS

Goans celebrate a wealth of holidays and festivals, though in practice even public holidays see shops, restaurants and the like open for business. See p21 for information on festivals and public holidays.

WHEN TO GOA

Goa's tourist season runs from late October to late April, with the high season extending from December to February. Throughout this time, there's no rainfall, days are dependably sunny, seas are calm and nights are balmy.

Outside this period, most beach huts and shacks are dismantled, and many hotels, shops and restaurants close down completely. This is all done in preparation for the monsoon, which scours Goa's shores (with hours, and sometimes days, of unbroken rainfall) between June and September. Few tourists visit during the monsoon, since the seas are rough, power cuts are frequent and tourist facilities are at a bare minimum, but this is when Goa is at its greenest and, without the tourist droves, most relaxed and traditional.

INTERNET

Internet cafes are widely available at almost every Goan beach destination, and access usually ranges from Rs 40 to Rs 60 per hour. Wifi access is slowly becoming more common, though it's rarely free: you'll likely pay upwards of Rs 100 per hour for the privilege, and far more at top-end hotels. Even the smallest internet outlets frequently offer printing, CD-writing facilities and other services to complement your usual surfing.

The following are useful web resources:

Goa Herald (www.oheraldo.in)
Goa Tourism Development Company (www.goa-tourism.com)
Goa World (www.goa-world.com)
GoaCom (www.goacom.com)
Radio Goa (www.radiogoa.net)

MONEY

Goa's economy revolves around the rupee (Rs), and ATMs are today so prevalent in Goa that this is your best source of cash, keeping aside some foreign currency for emergency exchange, or travellers cheques for back-up.

Accommodation costs in Goa are seasonal, with prices rising steeply during high season (November to April) and hitting rock bottom in the monsoon months between June and September. At Christmas and New Year, even high-season rates can double or triple.

Stays in Goa can be as cheap and cheerful or sky-high as you like: a simple *bhaji-pau* (a small, spicy curry) breakfast costs just Rs 8 and a local bus ride rarely costs more than Rs 20. A five-star hotel room might set you back Rs 50,000 or more; beach-hut accommodation varies from Rs 200 to Rs 2000 per night, depending on levels of comfort and facilities. Lunch at a local Goan joint costs around Rs 30; a drinkable bottle of wine costs Rs 450, and a day's self-drive car rental can be had for Rs 600.

ORGANISED TOURS

The **Goa Tourism Development Company** (GTDC; www.goa-tourism.com) offers a host of whirlwind tours of Goa, for those short on time and long on must-see lists; check its website for details. Most beach destinations have their fair share of boat-trip operators, offering daytrips to otherwise inaccessible beaches to spot dolphins, or along the state's lazy rivers. Check individual destination listings for the best of the bunch.

TELEPHONE

Mobile phones are common throughout Goa, and your own mobile phone will likely work whilst in Goa, though call costs are unsurprisingly excessive. Though cheap international calls can still be made at the many internet cafes, which will also have a STD/ISD phone booth or two, many visitors opt to purchase a local SIM card with prepaid credit. You can do this from many internet cafes and mobile-phone shops; it costs around Rs 700, plus the cost of 'unlocking' your phone if it's not already done. If you feel like investing, the most basic model of Nokia phone (usefully equipped with flashlight) comes in at Rs 1000. Bring along two passport photos of yourself, and a copy of your passport and visa. Note that SIM cards won't work outside Goa, except for receiving calls and sending text messages.

COUNTRY & STATE CODES

To dial Goa from outside India, use the country code (☎ 91), followed by Goa's state code (☎ 0832), leaving out the '0'. From inside India, use the full state code.

TIPPING

There's no official policy on tipping in India, though it's always appreciated as a supplement to waiters' wages – 10% of a bill is absolutely acceptable. The exception to this rule is five-star international hotels, where tipping hotel porters is the norm, as is the case elsewhere in the world. Taxi drivers don't need to be tipped, but if you've hired the driver for the day, it's generally a good idea to add on a little extra as a courtesy for getting you safely home.

TOURIST INFORMATION

The Goan Tourism Development Company (left) and the **Indian Ministry of Tourism** (www.incredibleindia.org) are both good sources of tourist information, as are the web resources listed under Internet (opposite).

TRAVELLERS WITH DISABILITIES

There are few provisions made in Goa for travellers with impaired mobility, except at top-end resorts, many of which have the advantage of wheelchair-accessible ground-floor rooms spread over gently landscaped grounds with wide walkways. Footpaths, lifts, toilets and the like are rarely, if ever, designed to accommodate wheel-chairs, and streets are littered with obstacles. However, these difficul-ties aren't insurmountable, and Goan people – including guides, taxi drivers and waiters – are extremely friendly and willing to help. For information specific to Goa, go to **Disability Goa** (www.disability goa.com), or contact **Timeless Excursions** (www.timelessexcursions.com), which arranges Indian holidays and tours for travellers with disabilities.

>INDEX

See also separate subindexes for See (p159), Do (p157), Shop (p160), Eat (p158), Drink (p158) and Play (p159).

000 map pages

🏃 DO

SHOP

000 map pages